HIGH PERFORMING CULTURE

Creating culture *intentionally*

Back in 2011, I sat down to write the book you're now holding. It was a chance for me to collect in one place many of the lessons I had learned, and taught, during my leadership career. To be honest, I thought of the book mostly as a "closure" step – an attempt to finish my old career before embarking on whatever the future might hold. Little did I know it would, in fact, become much more than that.

Instead, this book turned out to be a launching pad, rather than a closure step. Over the past several years, I've conducted hundreds of workshops and worked with scores of companies, teaching them the principles and the methods I originally created and later wrote about here. I've also founded a new company, High Performing Culture, with new products, tools, software, and a team of consultants helping companies across the country to be more intentional and systematic with their culture.

It's been gratifying to see so many thousands of people reading this book, and more importantly, gaining insights and wisdom they can put to use right away at work and at home. I hope it'll hold the same magic for you, and that, like so many others, you'll share it generously with your friends, family, and business associates.

Warmly,

David Friedman
Founder and CEO

HighPerformingCulture.com

Fundamentally
Different

David J. Friedman

∞ INFINITY
PUBLISHING

Copyright © 2011 by David J. Friedman

ISBN 978-1-4958-0894-4

Published August 2011

INFINITY PUBLISHING
1094 New DeHaven Street, Suite 100
West Conshohocken, PA 19428-2713
Toll-free (877) BUY BOOK
Local Phone (610) 941-9999
Fax (610) 941-9959
Info@buybooksontheweb.com
www.buybooksontheweb.com

CONTENTS

INTRODUCTION 1

INSTITUTIONALIZING VALUES 7

A BRIEF HISTORY 29

SECTION 1 – Core Values 33

    FUNDAMENTAL #1
    Do what's best for the client. 35
    FUNDAMENTAL #2
    Check the ego at the door. 41
    FUNDAMENTAL #3
    Practice A+ness as way of life. 48
    FUNDAMENTAL #4
    Take the extra time to do things right the first time. 55
    FUNDAMENTAL #5
    Seek to create win/win solutions. 58
    FUNDAMENTAL #6
    Practice blameless problem solving. 63
    FUNDAMENTAL #7
    Make decisions that reflect a reverence for long-term
    relationships. 70
    FUNDAMENTAL #8
    Maintain a solution orientation rather than a problem
    orientation. 76
    FUNDAMENTAL #9
    Work from the assumption that people are good, fair,
    and honest. 81
    FUNDAMENTAL #10
    Keep things fun. 90

SECTION 2 – Focus on Service 95

FUNDAMENTAL #11
Create a feeling of warmth and friendliness in every
client interaction. 97
FUNDAMENTAL #12
Practice the "Human Touch." 106
FUNDAMENTAL #13
Communicate to be understood. 115
FUNDAMENTAL #14
Set and ask for expectations. 122
FUNDAMENTAL #15
Make voicemail a valuable tool. 133
FUNDAMENTAL #16
Follow-up everything. 138
FUNDAMENTAL #17
Be punctual. 142

SECTION 3 – The Collaborative Way...............................147

FUNDAMENTAL #18
Listen generously. 149
FUNDAMENTAL #19
Speak straight. 158
FUNDAMENTAL #20
Be for each other. 168
FUNDAMENTAL #21
Honor commitments. 174
FUNDAMENTAL #22
Be a source for acknowledgement and appreciation. 182

SECTION 4 – Personal Effectiveness 191

FUNDAMENTAL #23
  Take responsibility. 193
FUNDAMENTAL #24
  Appearance counts. 207
FUNDAMENTAL #25
  Being organized makes a difference. 213
FUNDAMENTAL #26
  Double-check all work. 221
FUNDAMENTAL #27
  Look ahead and anticipate. 226
FUNDAMENTAL #28
  Have a bias for structure and rebar. 231
FUNDAMENTAL #29
  *The quality of your answers is directly related to the
  quality of your questions.* 240
FUNDAMENTAL #30
  Be quick to ask and slow to judge. 248

CONCLUSION..257

AFTERWORD...259

APPENDIX A
  The Original Fundamentals Card..............................261
APPENDIX B
  Initial e-mail introducing the Fundamentals...........262
APPENDIX C
  Transition e-mail with thoughts & observations ...264
APPENDIX D
  RSI Annual Fundamentals survey.............................267
APPENDIX E
  Book References...272

ACKNOWLEDGEMENTS...276

INTRODUCTION

Imagine, if you will, a crew of eight superbly conditioned athletes about to compete in a championship regatta. As the tension builds, they approach the starting line, eager to test themselves against the competition. The starting horn pierces the silence and they take off, rowing smoothly and strongly. They've trained and practiced together for years, and the absolute synchronicity of their timing is the proof. They row as one, practically gliding through the water, faster and faster, as if they're just skimming the surface. They're a finely-tuned team, speeding relentlessly toward their goal.

Highly effective organizations function in much the same way. Have you ever worked in such a place? Where everyone set aside their egos and worked cohesively as a team to achieve a common objective? If so, do you remember how much easier it was to get things done? How much faster you were able to accomplish a goal? How much more quickly problems were resolved and obstacles were overcome? If you've had this experience, you no doubt recognize how rewarding (and fun) it is to work as part of a highly functioning group.

But perhaps you're one of the millions of people who are stuck in organizations where people seem to work at cross purposes, like a rowing team where the timing of the oarsmen is out of sync, creating unnecessary choppiness and slowing progress toward the goal. Where people's personal agendas take precedence over team objectives. Where mistrust and cynicism are the norm. Where the company's stated vision, mission, and values are nothing but a framed poster in the Boardroom or a page on the website, with little to no relevance on a daily basis.

In my 27-year business career, I've had the opportunity to interact with several thousand companies, of all types and sizes, in nearly every industry imaginable. I've seen highly functioning organizations, and I've seen completely dysfunctional ones. I've spent years observing the differences and trying to determine the single most important factor that explains why organizations function the way they do. I'd like to share with you what I've learned.

My conclusions, however, are not simply those of a distant spectator, voyeuristically peeking behind the curtains of other organizations. Rather, they've been tested, refined, and honed by personal experience in my own company, as well as by my experience assisting other companies' leadership teams.

Personal Experience

From 1993-2008, I had the good fortune to lead the development of the company I co-founded, RSI, from a small family insurance agency into one of the largest and most successful independently-owned employee benefits firms in the country. During that time, we achieved success in nearly every important dimension of business. We grew revenues and profits at an average rate in excess of 20% per year. We were 7-time winners of Best Places to Work awards in NJ and in the Greater Philadelphia area. In 2006, we won the NJ Governor's Award for Performance Excellence, the highest award for quality available in the state. We won awards for leadership and for customer service. Our success at hiring the candidates we wanted exceeded 98%, and our staff turnover was consistently below 10%. Our customer service satisfaction was over 97%. In short, we had become one of those highly functioning organizations.

So, what was the cornerstone of our success at RSI that I also observed was the most important predictor of success in other companies? It was *organizational culture*. Quite simply, the culture of an organization is the one factor that most directly correlates to its effectiveness and, ultimately, its success.

"Its culture," you ask? "What about its sales strategy? Or its use of capital? Or its management team? Surely these must be more important than its culture." Let me show you why the culture is so vital to success.

Culture Drives Behavior

After years of observation and personal experience, it's abundantly clear to me that an organization's culture, more than any other single factor, is responsible for influencing the behavior of its people; and it's the behavior of its people on a day-to-day basis that most influences whether or not the organization reaches its goals. No matter how brilliant the strategy or how skilled the management team, how people perform their everyday tasks is what really determines success.

Think about the hundreds, thousands, and sometimes even millions of daily tasks performed by any organization—from putting together a sales presentation to answering a tech support call, from working an assembly line to pulling a product to be shipped, from delivering the right product to a customer to creating an invoice. Now imagine the difference between doing every one of these tasks at an exceptional level and doing every one of them with poor quality. A company's work is the sum total of all the seemingly mundane tasks completed on a daily basis by all of its workers. And how well these tasks are accomplished is driven by its culture, more so than by any other factor.

To be sure, every organization, whether by design or by accident, has a specific culture. It's evident the minute you walk into the building, in every customer interaction, in every written document, even in how the phones are answered. So what do we really mean by "culture"? While we all have a sense of an organization's culture, it can be hard to define precisely. Let me offer a working definition that I've developed over time and that I've found to be particularly useful. I define an organization's culture as

> The commonly-held set of values and principles that *shows up in the everyday behavior* of its people.

Notice that I've italicized the most important part of this definition: the idea that the culture is seen in the behavior of the people. The reason this distinction is so important is that many times a company will describe its culture according to a beautifully-crafted statement of values, but its people behave in ways that bear little resemblance to that statement. Behavior is the manifestation of culture in action.

To be clear, I'm not suggesting that values are not linked to behavior. In fact, it's quite the opposite. Our values govern our behavior. What I *am* suggesting is that the values we write on our websites are not always the ones that are operating inside our companies. Since we always act upon our values, the values that are truly inherent in our organizations are best recognized by observing the behavior of our people. They demonstrate the values every day by their actions with customers, with vendors, and with each other.

Now let's examine this notion in the context of my observations and experience with both highly effective organizations and dysfunctional ones. In highly effective organizations, there is a high degree of consistency between the values espoused by leadership and those demonstrated by the behavior of the people. In contrast, dysfunctional organizations are characterized by significant dissonance between stated values and observed behavior. More accurately, sometimes the behavior of the people would indicate that an entirely different set of values is in operation. Other times, there literally are no stated values. How does this happen? Often it's simply a failure on the part of leadership to promote the values effectively, while other times it's a failure to even recognize the opportunity to influence behavior through values.

Institutionalizing Values

So how do highly effective organizations create this consistency between stated values and observed behavior? They do it through a very specific set of actions that all serve to *institutionalize* their stated values. In other words, they intentionally take actions that serve to make their stated values an everyday part of the fabric of how they operate. The values become part of their very DNA, and as such, they show up in the observed behavior of the people. Effective organizations understand the power of this connection and they're *intentional* about creating that connection and harnessing that power.

In my years at RSI, we understood this power. We created a specific list of 30 values, known as The Fundamentals, which became the cornerstone of our culture. More importantly, we took the necessary steps to institutionalize these values. We learned largely by trial and error, constantly experimenting with new ways to promote and live our values. Convinced as I was of its importance, we were uncompromising in our commitment to this process. This book is a compilation of what I learned along the way.

In the ensuing chapters, here's what I'll share with you:

1. The 8 keys to institutionalizing any set of organizational values,
2. Specific examples of how we implemented each of the 8 keys,
3. An in-depth discussion of each of our 30 Fundamentals, and
4. Stories of how these Fundamentals impacted people both personally and professionally.

If you're a leader, it's my hope that this book will provide the inspiration and the tools for you to be more intentional in making values a bigger part of the organization you lead. If you take on this challenge, improved effectiveness and greater success will surely follow.

For everyone who reads this, whether you lead an organization, lead a family, or simply lead a life, it's my hope that some of these Fundamentals will find their way into your daily routines and that this book will inspire you to live your life in a way that's more consistent with the values that are most important to you.

David Friedman, 2011

INSTITUTIONALIZING VALUES

The 8 Key Steps

One of the hallmarks of fabulously successful companies is an aligned corporate culture. By this I mean that 1) there is a high degree of consistency between the organization's stated values and the behavior of its people, and 2) there is an equally high degree of consistency in the behavior observed among different workgroups throughout the organization. How is this consistency achieved? Through the intentional application of 8 key steps to institutionalizing the organization's most important values. In this chapter we'll examine each of these steps and I'll share examples of how we successfully implemented them at RSI.

The 8 steps to institutionalizing values are as follows:

1. Defining
2. Selecting
3. Integrating
4. Making visible
5. Using ritual
6. Coaching
7. Leading by example
8. Creating accountability

Let's take a look at them one at a time.

Defining

It sounds patently obvious that before you can make values an integral part of your organization you must clearly define what those values are. You'd be surprised, however, by the number of organizations that do not have any clear, written statement of operating values. If you don't currently have written values, or you feel the ones you have are outdated or irrelevant, here are a few suggestions on creating new ones.

I'm not a proponent of values development being a collaborative process where you get the input of all your "stakeholders." Rather, I think it's one of the essential roles of leadership to declare the organization's values. As such, the values should be ones that are deeply meaningful to you as the leader—ones that you have a strong conviction for and a robust passion about. Don't let an outside consultant develop a stylish, politically correct set of values for you; for if the values lack your passion, you'll never be able to successfully drive them through your organization.

The best place to start defining your values is by thinking about the things in which you believe strongly. What principles have you built your life upon? What advice are you always giving people about how things ought to be done? What behavior do you wish you saw more frequently around you? Ideally, you'll have between 4 and 10 important values that you can identify. While at RSI we had 30, and it worked particularly well for us, I think having that many values can be unwieldy for most organizations.

Each value should be accompanied by a statement or two that explains what you mean by that value. More specifically, the statement should describe what behavior that value calls for. Let me give you some examples. If one of your values is "friendliness," you might have a statement that says, "Greet all customers with a smile and use their name whenever possible. Make dealing with you a happy experience." If one of your values is "teamwork," you might have a statement that says, "Look for opportunities to help each other, even when it's outside your job function."

Here's a great example of using explanatory statements. The card below is part of a staff pledge from the YMCA of Burlington and Camden Counties, in New Jersey. Notice how clearly the card describes the expected behaviors.

DRESS FOR SUCCESS
I will create a friendly experience for our members. *I will always wear my nametag* so that members can clearly identify I am available to help.

SMILE AND SAY HELLO
I will provide a warm welcome for our members. I *will promptly and courteously acknowledge members, make eye contact, smile and say hello to everyone,* including children and teens. I will try to learn our member's name. *Better yet,* I will introduce members to each other.

MEET AND GREET
I will make a personal connection with our members. I *will introduce myself to at least one new member every day.* I *will lend members a hand.* I will become the person they can feel comfortable talking to when they have a question or concern. A member should never feel like they are wasting my time.

SEE IT, OWN IT
If I see it, I own it. I *will take responsibility for correcting the problems I see,* be they as small as a piece of paper on the floor or as large as a member complaint.

GIVE THANKS
I will be grateful. Every member has chosen to spend part of their day with us. I *will thank all our volunteers every time they lend a hand.* I *will take time to thank or offer a sincere compliment to another staff person each time I work.*

HAVE FUN
I will have fun everyday when I come to the YMCA.

YMCA Character Development

Statements like these help your people to understand what it looks like to behave in a way that's consistent with the named value. Most importantly, they help people to see the connection between values and behavior. They begin to understand that values aren't something relegated to a poster, but rather they're a prescription for everyday action.

At RSI, I wrote a list of 30 Fundamentals to serve as a guide for our behavior. (In the next chapter, I'll share with you the story of how I came up with this idea.) To be fair, some of our Fundamentals might accurately be called "values" while others might better be described as "practices." They're listed in Appendix A. You'll note that they're divided into 4 groupings: Core Values, Focus on Service, The Collaborative Way, and Personal Effectiveness. Each Fundamental is composed of a statement that calls for a particular type of behavior, and then has one or more sentences that further clarify its intention. Notice how crafting it this way makes it easy to understand just what behavior is expected; and when everyone has the same expectation, it becomes far easier to create a consistent culture.

The more clearly your values are stated, and the more fully you've described the related expected behavior, the more successfully you'll make those values come alive on a daily basis.

Selecting

In his best-selling book <u>Good to Great</u>, Jim Collins talks about the importance of "getting the right people on the bus." If you don't have the right people, you're not going to get where you want to go. This is abundantly clear to me as it relates to culture and values.

To be candid, I don't believe that you can have much success getting people who don't believe in your core values to consistently behave in accordance with them. Experience tells me that most people in our organizations come to us with a set of values, developed throughout their lifetimes, that are pretty well formed. Either those values match nicely with our own, or they don't; and if they don't, you're not going to have much luck in changing them. So what's the implication of this in relation to institutionalizing values? You have to be uncompromising in selecting and bringing in people you believe are already a good values fit for your organization.

In the early stages of this effort, it's not uncommon to find that a fair percentage of your current staff does not embody the values you're trying to promote. I'm often asked how to handle this conflict. My experience is that "non-compliant" people usually fit into two categories: some are simply neutral, non-supporters, while others are actually subversive. The subversive ones are essentially working against you. Their cynicism is poisonous and can destroy your best efforts from within. They often have a point-of-view or a way of acting that they're heavily invested in protecting, even if it serves to undermine the success of the organization. Be aware of the impact that these people have on others. What message are you sending to the rest of your group when you allow counterproductive behavior to continue without consequence? While it may sound harsh, these people need to be removed from your organization as quickly as possible. High performance is impossible with them on the team.

The other category of non-compliant people, the more neutral ones, will ultimately leave of their own accord. As you begin to purposely hire more and more people who are a good values fit, those who don't fit slowly become a smaller and smaller minority. They begin to recognize that they're not like others, their sphere of influence tends to diminish, and they become more disgruntled. Incidentally, expect to hear things like "This place isn't the same anymore," and "I don't know what's happening around here," and "This company doesn't get it" as they prepare for their departure. No one leaves a company saying, "This is a fabulous organization that's destined to achieve great things, but I just don't fit in."

The key here is that great organizations know the importance of bringing in the "right" people—not just those with the right skills and experience, but those with the right attitudes. To be clear, I'm not suggesting that you should hire people who don't have the requisite skills to do the job you're looking to fill. The right skills or experience is a necessary but not sufficient condition for hiring. The candidate must also demonstrate the right value system. How do you determine this?

At RSI, we used several methods for ascertaining the values fit of a candidate. First, we designed interview questions around our values. These questions were always behavior-oriented. For example, high-touch customer service was a cornerstone of our organization. We might ask a candidate to tell a story about a time that they either gave or received extraordinary service. If they couldn't come up with a good story, or they told it with no passion, they likely didn't "get" customer service. Conversely, if their face lit up as they excitedly told an amazing story, then customer service was likely to be in their DNA. Since one of our Fundamentals is about being well-organized, we might ask a candidate to describe the system they used to manage their tasks or to describe how they organized their desk. How they answered this question revealed a tremendous amount about how they approached organization. If their idea of organization was having post-it notes all around their desk as reminders, then they weren't our person. Here again, my experience is that I can take a generally organized person and give them better tools and support to enhance this trait, but I cannot take a totally disorganized person and make them organized.

Another method we used to get data about values fit was to have a candidate spend time (often over a lunch) meeting with a group of current staff. We'd ask our staff to give us feedback about certain aspects of the fit. We found that as our culture grew stronger and more defined, our staff became more and more protective of it, and they became heavily invested in making sure we brought in the right type of people.

Throughout this book, I'll sometimes use the word "uncompromising" to describe our approach to an effort. When I use that word, I mean it quite literally. In other words, I mean "with no exception." This kind of rigor is necessary, because without it, too many quite reasonable excuses arise, and eventually the quality of what you're trying to accomplish becomes hopelessly degraded.

With regard to selection, we were uncompromising in our commitment to hire only people we believed to be a strong values fit for our organization. That doesn't mean that we didn't make mistakes. In hiring, one never bats 1.000. On a few occasions we misread some signs or failed to pick up on others and therefore made a poor hire; but this was rare, and we quickly corrected the mistake. Moreover, the mistake was in our judgment, not in our commitment.

I should also point out that determining a candidate is not a good fit for your organization does not suggest they're somehow not a great person. They may be a wonderful and skilled person who simply would be a better fit in another organization. While diversity may be a good thing from the standpoint of background or experience, I want homogeneity when it comes to values. It's the only way to build the consistent link between values and behavior that sets truly outstanding organizations apart.

Integrating

After having established a clear, written set of values and corresponding behaviors, and after turning up the rigor around selecting only those people who are assessed to be a good fit, the next key to institutionalizing your values is what I call "integration." Integration is similar to what some companies call "orientation" or, more recently, "on-boarding." Whatever word you choose, it's the process whereby a new recruit goes from being an "outsider" to becoming an "insider." At RSI, we used the word "integration" because it implied that the new person was becoming a part of us, versus simply learning about us.

For most recruits, the integration process is the first formal introduction to all important aspects of the company. This is a critical time to talk about and demonstrate values. The time and attention you place on values during integration sends a crystal clear message to all people, new and old, about how important these truly are to your organization. If our corporate values get no more than a cursory mention, if any at all, how can we expect our people to take them seriously?

Through the years, we developed and refined an award-winning, best-in-class integration program that never ceased to amaze new employees. It was a one- to two-week program that covered everything a new person needed to know, from our culture and values to our history, from our strategy to our finances, from learning people's names to learning how to work the phone system. As with other aspects of our approach, it was *uncompromising*. Every person in every department began their career with the full integration every time. No exceptions.

In every case, as the President, I met with each new group of employees, on the first morning of their very first day, and spent two full hours with them talking about our culture and values, and the importance of our Fundamentals. I literally went through each of the 30 Fundamentals and explained the expected behaviors that were imbedded in each one, giving specific examples to illustrate their relevance to our everyday work. This proved to be powerful on several levels. Most directly, I was able to make sure that every person understood the behavioral expectations clearly. Just as important, however, was the secondary message I was sending. The very fact that the President of the company took the time to address this in such detail on the first day spoke volumes about its importance to our organization.

This same multi-level impact is evident, whether we recognize it or not, through any integration process. First is the impact of what you say directly, if anything, about your values. But at the same time, how you handle your integration process is one of the first opportunities your organization has to demonstrate its values in action. Are you well-organized? Do things happen on time? Are you prepared? Are people friendly? Do others in the organization seem committed to integration? How do people react to newcomers? Are they welcoming or are they standoffish? As always, your actions speak louder than your words. Make sure your actions are in line with the values you espouse, for people can easily spot insincerity.

At the end of our integration process, we asked employees to complete a self-assessment where they responded to a number of questions indicating how well they absorbed what we intended. There was also space for them to describe some of what they noticed most or were most impressed by. Following are some actual quotes from just a handful of employees. These were typical and were representative of the impact not only of integration, but of the way in which values were conveyed:

- "I was impressed by many things but the most important was the company's culture. It is truly amazing how much effort is taken during the recruiting process to find employees who are the right cultural fit for RSI."

- "Any company can explain their vision, mission, and values, but I was impressed to find that the Fundamentals were actually practiced by all RSI employees."

- "During orientation I was most impressed with the Fundamentals and the way they are put into practice each and every day. The Fundamentals are not simply a list, but instead they are representative of the company and its beliefs."

- "The culture created within this organization is one I heard a great deal about during the interview process, but even still, would never have imagined it being so real and complete."

- "I have been most impressed with RSI's culture and how each employee actually fits the culture. It is continually practiced by everyone, including the executive management, which I feel is very important."

- "Through Integration and additional conversations I've had with RSI employees, I am 100% confident that we are accurate reflections of the RSI Fundamentals."

- "I have been most impressed with the unified culture that has been promoted here. Everyone truly believes and adheres to this code, and that is extremely impressive."

I simply cannot overstate the impact of an effectively done integration process.

To be sure, whether you're aware or not, you begin to send messages about your values with the very first contact a potential recruit has with your organization. How are they treated on the phone? If they come in, what does your lobby look like? Do people smile? Does someone greet strangers, and if so, how? How is the interview process handled? How do you handle follow-up contact with job candidates? All of these experiences tell a candidate about the culture and values of your organization. Highly effective teams manage every aspect of the relationship, starting with the very first contact, to demonstrate consistency with stated values.

In addition to the attention we gave to treating candidates with care throughout the recruitment process, the introduction of our values began in earnest even before a new hire's first day. Once a hiring decision had been made, I would send a personal, hand-written note to each new recruit, at their home, in which I would welcome them and let them know how much I was looking forward to working with them. (See Fundamental #12 – Practice the "Human Touch.") The fact that the President of the company knew they were coming and would take the time to write them a personal note always had a significant impact on people. It once again demonstrated a number of the values I wanted them to understand and, in turn, practice. Following that note, they would also get several other pieces of mail from me prior to their first day, each with a handwritten message. One of those pieces was our Fundamentals card (See Appendix A), on which are listed the 30 Fundamentals and their descriptions. I would ask each person to review them prior to the first day, as we'd be spending considerable time on them when they arrive. Once again, I was sending them an important message about where the Fundamentals existed in our corporate priorities.

Not all companies have the time or resources to develop and carry out an integration process as thoroughly as we did at RSI. However, regardless of the length or the sophistication of their process, all effective organizations recognize the critical opportunity that integration provides to not only *tell* new people about the values but to *demonstrate* them as well.

Making Visible

While posting your values in places that are easy to see does not in and of itself cause people to adhere to them, it's nonetheless important for everyone to see regular reminders. It's hard for most of us to remember to put our values into action if we're not confronted with them very often. There are infinite ways this can be accomplished.

At RSI, our Fundamentals were printed on folded cards that everyone could carry with them in their wallet, their pocket, or their purse. I kept one copy in my breast pocket every day. We created mouse pads with the Fundamentals for everyone to keep at their desk. We also created 30 artistically-framed photo prints that depicted each of our Fundamentals, and these prints lined the hallways of our office. As I'll describe more fully in the next section, we focused on a particular Fundamental each week. The Fundamental of the Week was posted on an easel in our front lobby, and each manager had the week's Fundamental printed in a Lucite frame that sat in their office. A framed print of the Fundamentals hung in our main conference room and, of course, they were listed on our website.

Giving the Fundamentals such high visibility helped keep them present in our minds and showed people they were important. It also made it easier to remember to use the language of our Fundamentals in our daily conversations because they were all around us. Highly effective organizations make their most important tenets visible for all to see.

Using Ritual

The creation and maintenance of rituals can play a critically important role in keeping our values more present in our minds. Here are a couple of examples with which everyone is familiar.

Think about the ritual of playing the Star Spangled Banner before every athletic contest. I'm continually amazed and impressed at the impact it has on most Americans, even though it's become so routine. Most people will become silent, they'll take off their hats, and many will put their right hand over their heart. For just a few moments, the playing of our national anthem causes us to reflect on the good fortune we have to be Americans and generates in us a feeling of patriotism. It connects us, even for just a few minutes, with each other, and to the values that this country is based upon.

Think about the ritual that many families have of saying a prayer of thanks prior to eating a meal. We stop what we're doing and thinking about for just a few moments and briefly pause to reflect upon that for which we're thankful. We think about what's important to us.

Now, there's no reason we can't think patriotic thoughts on our own, and we certainly can always take time out to be thankful, but the reality is that without some activity that forces us to do so, we rarely stop what we're doing long enough to reflect in meaningful ways. Rituals can create an automatic, non-thinking way of making this happen. When I say "non-thinking" here I don't mean devoid of thought; rather I mean that it doesn't require mental effort to remember to do it because the ritual supplies the impetus. We don't have to remember to think patriotic thoughts or even to play the national anthem, because it automatically happens prior to every athletic event. The same is true for a pre-meal prayer. The event of a meal creates the automatic response to conduct the prayer. So, how does this concept relate to institutionalizing organizational values?

I first got turned onto the value of ritual by Ritz-Carlton. Indeed, as you'll learn in the next chapter, exposure to the Ritz-Carlton Basics is what gave me the idea to develop our Fundamentals. Ritz-Carlton is one of the finest, most effective, best-run companies in the world. In fact, it was the first two-time winner of the Malcolm Baldrige Quality Award, the highest recognition for quality achievement available for an American company.

Imagine the challenges of creating a consistent, values-based organizational culture when you have more than 32,000 employees working at 78 different properties in 23 countries. To make it even more difficult, imagine accomplishing this with a workforce that ranges from sales people to front desk personnel to housekeepers to cooks. Ritz-Carlton uses all 8 of the keys to institutionalizing values that I'm describing, and the most vital to their success is ritual.

Of all the Ritz-Carlton rituals, none has more far-reaching impact than the Daily Lineup. Every day, in every shift, in every department, in every property (including the corporate office), team members gather to begin the shift with the Daily Lineup. It's typically a 10 to 20-minute meeting where the Basic of the Day is reviewed, and where important messages are disseminated corporate-wide and property-wide. I've had the chance to personally witness several Daily Lineups, and it's inspiring to see both the commitment to the process as well as the effect of it.

Even in the corporate headquarters, Daily Lineup takes place each morning at the same time. Everyone knows not to be on the phone or busy at that time because attendance is not optional! There's even a standard way that all guests are welcomed (I was a guest at one of these Lineups). It may sound trite or "hokey," but I assure you it's anything but. Ritz-Carlton has harnessed the power of ritual to effectively drive a consistent culture across an immense and varied workforce.

Another great example of the use of ritual is at Aetna. For many years I served on Aetna's National Broker Advisory Council. For me, the best part of this service was the opportunity to get to know Aetna's President and CEO at the time, Ron Williams. Ron is without question one of the greatest leaders I've had the privilege to observe.

Ron believed strongly in the power of organizational culture and values, so much so that he made them central to everything he did. Under his guidance, Aetna developed a set of values they called The Aetna Way. Ron established a ritual of starting every single presentation, no matter who the audience, external or internal, by reviewing the Aetna Way and talking about its importance to everything they do. I watched him do this time after time, much like beginning a meeting with the Pledge of Allegiance or a game with the Star Spangled Banner. While Ron has since retired, the ritual continues to be practiced by Aetna's current President, Mark Bertolini.

At RSI, we used several rituals to deepen our practice of the Fundamentals. The first was the weekly lesson for the Fundamental of the Week. Each week, we focused our attention on one particular Fundamental. We started with Fundamental #1 in the first week (when I began the process), and cycled through them in order every week for 30 weeks. In the 31st week, we would go back to #1 again and begin the process anew. During the first 30 weeks, each Sunday night I would send an e-mail and a voicemail to all employees with the Fundamental of the Week and a short lesson explaining some nuance to it, an example of it in practice, or some other aspect I wanted people to understand. I used these lessons to help people make the connection between the Fundamental and its applicability to our daily lives at work.

At the end of the first 30 weeks, I passed the responsibility for the weekly lesson to my management team. Each member of the team would take a week to author the message to be disseminated to the staff. This helped the management team to take greater ownership of the Fundamentals, and helped the staff to gain additional perspectives outside my own. This went on for the second 30 weeks.

As we began to approach our third cycle of 30 weeks, I passed the responsibility to our staff at large. We posted a sign-up sheet and asked employees to choose a week to author the lesson for their peers. As you can imagine, this took ownership of the Fundamentals to an entirely different level as it became an organization-wide behavioral norm rather than a leadership initiative. This weekly ritual, more than any single thing we did, helped connect our values to our everyday performance.

In Appendix B, I've included the text of the e-mail I sent to our staff when I introduced the whole concept of the Fundamentals. In Appendix C, I've included the text of the e-mail I sent at the end of the first 30 weeks as I prepared to pass the responsibility to the management team. As you can see, I used the e-mail as another opportunity to share my thoughts on why our practice of the Fundamentals was so important.

Another important ritual we used to further our practice of the Fundamentals was to make the Fundamental of the Week be the first agenda item in every meeting. Whether it was a small team meeting, a departmental meeting, a management meeting, or an entire-company staff meeting, the first agenda item was always the Fundamental of the Week. The leader of the meeting would typically read the Fundamental and then share his or her personal thoughts about the principle. This might include a recent story where it applied or a subtlety that was often overlooked. Others would frequently chime in with their own thoughts, and a five to six-minute discussion of the Fundamental would ensue. This was a tremendously effective way to deepen people's understanding of each Fundamental.

The key issue to understand about the power of ritual is that by happening as a habit, it prevents us from forgetting. The Fundamental of the Week was our first agenda item not simply when we remembered to make it that, or not just when we had enough time. It was the first agenda item *every* time. That's what a ritual is all about. We don't play the national anthem only if it's convenient. We play it before *every* professional game.

Of the 8 keys, this one represents the greatest opportunity to link your values to your daily work life. The most effective organizations put this power to work for them.

Coaching

One of the most important ways people learn how values apply to daily action is through the coaching you provide to staff when faced with real-life situations. This is where you make values relevant.

The most effective way to connect people to your values when coaching is to use the specific language of those values. It's your chance to take the words down from the poster on the wall and show people how those words serve as a guide to taking appropriate actions.

This was a common practice for us at RSI. For example, suppose a staff member was rushing through paperwork to get it out the door without ensuring that it was as close to perfect as possible. We would offer them extra help and remind them that Fundamental #4 says to "Take the extra time to do things right the first time" and talk about why that's so important. If a staff member was struggling with how they were interpreting the actions of a difficult client or co-worker, we would reference Fundamental #9, which says that we "Work from the assumption that people are good, fair and honest." If we take this to be true, we can look at what else might be going on in the situation that we need to appreciate to better understand the other person's actions. The more we use the language of our values, the more real they become for people.

Another form of coaching we used was to do training based on case studies. We developed a series of typical scenarios that one might encounter at work. Some related to customer or supplier situations, while others were challenges among co-workers. We divided people into small groups and asked them to discuss a scenario, determine the appropriate course of action, and identify which Fundamental they would use to guide their behavior. This had the obvious effect of helping people to practice using the Fundamentals as a real-world tool.

Here's an important point to keep in mind about coaching: In highly effective organizations, values are never used as a tool to berate or punish someone. Rather, they're used to support each other in our effort to behave in a way that's consistent with our values.

This is subtle but important, so let me explain further. In *ineffective* organizations, people catch others falling short of the desired behavior and conclude that the "offender" doesn't believe in the value or has a lack of commitment to it. It's a cynical point of view that tends to tear others down.

In highly effective organizations, however, we believe in each other's commitment and we recognize that none of us is perfect. If we fall short, we depend on each other for support, guidance, and coaching to help us be the best we can be. We see lapses not as critical failures of commitment, but rather as opportunities for improvement. The goal isn't to prove that someone else is wrong. It's to get people to more consistently behave in ways that are an accurate reflection of our values.

Leading by Example

While rituals provide a structure for routinely connecting values to behavior, and coaching provides a way to make values relevant in the "real world," nothing speaks more loudly than the example set by the senior leaders of the organization. Both consciously and unconsciously, people look to their leaders for guidance about acceptable behavior. If you're a leader, you're on stage at every moment, so it's critical that you make the most of that opportunity.

Imagine a staff member comes to you looking for direction on how to handle a difficult client situation. The client is upset and looking for a resolution. If you tell your staff member not to worry about it because the client is always complaining anyway, you're demonstrating what you consider to be acceptable behavior for working with customers. Conversely, if you aggressively work with the person to find a solution and you promptly call the customer to acknowledge the issue and show them you care, you're also demonstrating what you consider to be acceptable. Don't ever forget, that for better or worse, your people pay far more attention to what you *do* than what you *say*. It matters not what's written on your walls or your website, but only what you actually do.

At RSI, it was a priority for us to be sure that our leaders were modeling our values. Not surprisingly, one of the anonymous survey questions asked on the annual Best Places to Work survey reads, "Senior leadership regularly models our organization's values." We were proud of the fact that during the many years we participated in that survey, our positive response rates to that question were always between 92% and 100%.

In high-functioning organizations, leaders recognize the role their example plays in modeling values. They use this to their advantage by regularly demonstrating behavior that's consistent with the organization's stated values.

Creating Accountability

The last of the 8 keys to institutionalizing values is the one most often overlooked, and yet it's one of the most important steps. If you're serious about wanting to be an accurate reflection of the values you espouse, then you have to find ways to hold yourselves accountable to that standard. Let me give you some examples of ways this can be done.

More and more companies are beginning to include a values component on annual performance reviews. This can be very effective in a number of ways. First, it forces you to describe your values in behavioral terms, for how else will you be able to evaluate whether or not someone is performing in a way consistent with them? Second, it forces a regular discussion between a manager and his or her direct reports about the organizational values and what they mean on a day-to-day basis. Third, including them in the performance review process demonstrates their importance to the organization. And fourth, having some incentives and consequences related to the degree of success in demonstrating behavior consistent with the values reinforces that behavior.

Another method we used at RSI was an annual survey based on our Fundamentals. The survey was sent to three different constituencies—our customers, our suppliers/vendors, and our own staff. For each Fundamental, I described what it would look like for us to behave in a way that was consistent with it. I then asked respondents to evaluate us in terms of the behavior they observed in our people. Did we "almost always, usually, sometimes, seldom, or never" act in this way? The results were tallied and then shared back with those who responded. The actual text of the RSI Annual Fundamentals Survey is included in Appendix D.

Conducting the survey sent a strong message, to both our people and those we came in contact with, that we were serious about the link between our values and our behavior. It served to keep us accountable to each other and to the world at large. I'm proud to say that of more than 10,000 total question responses, 97% described us as either usually or almost always demonstrating our values, and 72% said we almost always behaved this way.

Creating accountability for our actions is the part of the process that says "we mean it." Without this, performing in accordance with our values is just the "flavor of the month"—something for your staff to wait out until you get distracted and move on to some other new initiative. Highly effective organizations reinforce the seriousness of their efforts by building in accountability.

The steps that highly functioning organizations take to institutionalize their values are straightforward and clear. Though I've given you suggestions and examples from my own experience, you're limited only by your own creativity in how you implement those steps. Like the crew cutting speedily through the water, rowing in flawless synchronicity, so too can your team achieve greater degrees of effectiveness and success by developing and implementing an aligned organizational culture.

In the remainder of this book, I'll present in-depth discussions of each of our 30 Fundamentals. I've also asked members of my former staff, both management and non-management, to offer their personal stories of how they used a particular Fundamental or how it impacted them. It's my pleasure to share their stories with you.

But before I do so, I promised earlier to share with you my own story of the origin of the Fundamentals . . .

A BRIEF HISTORY

So how did all this start? The story begins in the fall of
2003. And it begins as a customer service story more than anything else. While RSI had always been known for amazing customer service, I simply wasn't satisfied that we were the best we
could be. I was intrigued by the legendary service stories of
companies like Nordstrom and Ritz-Carlton and Stew Leonard's
Grocery, and I wanted to know more about how these organizations created the culture that produced such consistent service
excellence. Quite honestly, I wanted to be more like them, and I
wanted to push the boundaries of our thinking about what's
possible.

A Brainstorming Event

Not sure how to go about getting us to that next level, I decided to schedule a brainstorming event for the entire organization (approximately 70-80 people at the time) where we could
open our minds more fully and dream about what truly extraordinary service might look like. To put us in the right frame of
mind, I decided it would be best to change the context and go
outside our normal office surroundings. As I thought about
where to go, I figured, "Where better than a Ritz-Carlton to fully
maximize the opportunity to think differently?" So I arranged
for us to have lunch at the Ritz-Carlton in Center City, Philadel-

phia, and then to spend the afternoon in a meeting room there doing brainstorming exercises.

To build the anticipation, the only thing I told our staff in advance was that we were going to close the office early on a particular Friday afternoon in December and that we'd be going somewhere as a group. I chartered two buses to take us to Philadelphia, and on the way over we played Joel Barker's famous video, The New Business of Paradigms, to jumpstart our thinking.

At this time, I knew very little about Ritz-Carlton as an organization other than their reputation for having the industry's best customer service. However, I was certain that the consistent behavior of their people—who created these service experiences—couldn't have been an accident. So I called the hotel, explained my goals for the day, and asked if there was someone who could talk to us during lunch to give us some insight into how Ritz-Carlton works behind the scenes. Not surprisingly, they were pleased to do so and they arranged for a woman in their HR department to speak with us. Little did I know, at the time, the impact that talk was to have.

The woman shared with us a few of the systems and processes used by Ritz-Carlton to create consistently extraordinary behavior. She talked about their method of noticing and recording guest preferences, their Daily Line-up that occurs in every shift in every property around the world and, most significantly for me, she talked about their 20 Basics.

The Ritz-Carlton Basics

The Ritz-Carlton Basics are a series of 20 behaviors that are taught to all staff. They include actions like "Each employee will continuously identify defects throughout the hotel," "Any employee who hears a customer complaint owns the complaint," and "Escort guests rather than pointing out directions to another area of the Hotel." But the key to why these are so powerful has little to do with the items themselves. Rather, it's how Ritz-Carlton *uses* the Basics to foster consistent behavior that is so remarkable.

The 20 Basics are listed in numerical order and printed on laminated cards that are carried by all staff. Each day, one of the Basics is featured in the Daily Line-up that occurs for every shift in every department. Here, the Basic of the day is reviewed and further explained. It's worth noting that if today is day #16, it's #16 for every Ritz-Carlton employee in every property (including the corporate headquarters) around the world. Every employee around the world participates in the Line-up and can tell you about today's Basic. (The next time you're at a Ritz-Carlton, ask any staff member what the Basic of the Day is and watch what happens. I've done this!) The Basics are covered in numerical order, and each 21st day, they go back to the beginning. In this way, an organization as large as Ritz-Carlton has managed to drive amazingly consistent behavioral performance.

As you might imagine, I was totally smitten with this concept. From early on in our business, I was searching for ways to make incredible service a predictable result rather than the lucky by-product of interacting with a particularly nice person. The idea of the 20 Basics lit a spark for me, and I went home that weekend and immediately began writing our "basics" and thinking about how to use them.

The RSI Fundamentals

As a starting point, we had 10 "core values" that I had written years before and had taught to all of our employees as they began their careers with us. We also had 5 Collaborative Way practices, which were a series of communication tools we had learned, taught, and incorporated into our work. I started to think about the many values, behaviors, and practices I had always taught over the years but had never codified in one place. During the next week or two, my list grew from 17 to 22 to 26 and eventually to 30.

I decided to call my list our "Fundamentals" because I felt they were the fundamental underpinning for a successful organization. For each Fundamental, I wrote a title, and then a two- or three-sentence description further clarifying its meaning and its applicability. As I reviewed the list, I tried to find some useful way of organizing the Fundamentals so that they would be easier to work with. Beyond those original core values and the Collaborative Way, I noticed that some of the Fundamentals were centered on specific ways to give extraordinary service, while others were more focused on personal effectiveness. And so I broke down the 30 as follows:

- Fundamentals 1-10: Core Values
- Fundamentals 11-17: Focus on Service
- Fundamentals 18-22: The Collaborative Way
- Fundamentals 23-30: Personal Effectiveness

Once this was complete, I gave it to our graphics firm to design our printed cards. I then began to consider how I wanted to introduce our newly created Fundamentals and, more importantly, how best to make them a part of our daily experience.

On February 22, 2004, I formally introduced the newly created Fundamentals to our organization in the e-mail found in Appendix B. What came next is the story of this book.

SECTION 1

Core Values – These values have been a corner-stone of our success for more than 20 years.

I penned these original core values back in the early '90s as part of a larger document I wrote to provide direction to our growing staff. At the time, we were implementing many changes throughout the organization, and I felt it was important to explain, in writing, what we were doing and where we were going. I've often found that in times of change it can be helpful to connect people to those things that are permanent and unchanging, like core values. It was the need for this solid foundation that led me to identify the most important principles on which we had been built.

Over the years, the document I wrote became known as our "teaching document," and the principles become known as our "core values." I reviewed this document and I taught the core values with every new employee during their integration, long before these values became known as the first ten of our Fundamentals.

FUNDAMENTAL #1

Do what's best for the client.

In all situations, act in the best interests of our client, even if it's to our own detriment. Our reputation for integrity is one of our greatest assets.

In Stephen M. R. Covey's fascinating book, <u>The Speed of Trust</u>, he makes a compelling case for the measurable impact that trust (or lack of trust) has on everything, from the quality of our relationships to the profitability of our companies. He identifies 13 behaviors that have been proven to generate trust (a number of which track closely with our Fundamentals), and he goes on to describe trust as existing in five "waves." The fourth of Covey's waves is "marketplace trust." This is the trust that a company creates with its customers and prospects, a notion that could also be called its *brand*, or even its *reputation*. Almost every successful company in the world identifies the value of its brand (its marketplace trust) as its most valuable asset.

Covey's research further reveals that one of the foundations of marketplace trust is the perception that the company is not merely out to make a profit, but rather that it genuinely wants to do what's best for the customer. There's a reason I made this the first of our Fundamentals. It truly is the foundation on which everything else is built.

Lessons Learned

I entered the insurance business in May of 1983, literally two days after my graduation from college. I had the good fortune to work in partnership with my father, who had spent most of his career in the industry. More than anything else, my father succeeded because he had high personal credibility. He had the ability to cause others to trust in him. In fact, many revered him. How did he do this? It was really quite simple. He was doggedly determined to always do what was best for them, and they knew it.

In those early days of my career, my father and I worked side-by-side and spent many hours discussing business. It's funny—I hear stories or read books about people who recall the pearls of wisdom their parents always used to spout. In my case, I remember very few things my parents "always used to say." To be sure, I learned many lessons; but they taught largely by example. However, the one thing I do distinctly remember my father teaching me overtly is the importance of *always* doing what's best for the client.

Putting Lessons Into Practice

We had many opportunities to put this lesson into practice at RSI. Our job was to help mostly small and mid-size companies purchase the right employee benefit products for their needs, and then we supported those products by acting as their benefits department. We were paid an ongoing commission by the insurance companies whose products we placed with that employer.

One of our primary functions was to annually review the insurance package, solicit competing bids, and then make recommendations to our client.

Since our commission was normally calculated as a percentage of the insurance premiums paid by the employer, saving our client money usually meant reducing our annual revenue. Sometimes we were also faced with situations where the best insurance carrier for a client was the one with the lowest commission schedule. My advice to our staff was always the same and was unequivocal. Do what's best for the client.

Sometimes doing what's best for the client involves giving them advice they don't want to hear, even at the risk of losing their business. I remember one time when a small client had been told by others that self-insuring their medical plan was a sure way to save money. We knew this made little

Last year, one of the clients I work with was faced with a difficult situation. They were experiencing a significant downturn in their business with no relief in sight, their health plan renewal increase was more than $100k, and there were no market alternatives. Though the client had a contentious relationship with their union, we suggested they at least consider a union-sponsored plan that we were familiar with through another client. This plan turned out to be an aggressively priced, rich benefit offering that represented a savings of more than $100k from their current plan and more than $200k from their renewal.

Though we were excluded from brokering the union deal and were therefore likely to lose the client revenue, we nonetheless strongly recommended they make the move. Under the circumstances, it was clearly the best decision for the client, and we knew that our first obligation was to do what was right for them. We may have lost the money now, but we added to our reputation for the future.
-Paul F.

sense given their small size and risk profile, and we were adamant in our determination to make the right recommendation. It would have been easy to simply go along with what they wanted to do, but it would also have been a betrayal of our responsibility. Ultimately, the employer chose to disregard our advice and we lost them as a client. If the situation happened again, we'd still handle it the same way. (Incidentally, that client eventually came back to us, and I have no doubt that it was, in part, a result of the respect we gained by our steadfastness in advocating for their best interest.)

One of my favorite books on this topic is by Patrick Lencioni. It's called <u>Getting Naked: A Business Fable About Shedding The Three Fears That Sabotage Client Loyalty</u>. The author uses the idea of nakedness to describe allowing ourselves to become vulnerable in our pursuit of serving the client. Notes Lencioni, "At its core, naked service boils down to the abil-

> *Several years ago, I was on a sales call with a large, self-insured prospect. It was a case we'd been cultivating for some time, and we finally had the chance to meet with the CFO. He was a pretty competent guy, and he was eager to share with me his view of how self-insurance works and where they should be looking to reduce cost. While some salespeople assume it's always best to agree with the prospect, I took a different approach.*
>
> *I figured my job was to help this person and to do what's best for him, regardless of whether I ultimately earned his business. He had some significant misconceptions about self-insurance that I needed to challenge and then correct. While disagreeing with a prospect can be risky, it was the only way to truly serve him. He didn't need a "yes" man. He needed someone who was looking out for him and would tell him the truth. In the end, I was able to help him see things differently and won his trust (and the business). To this day, he still talks about how much he appreciated my commitment to doing what was best for him.*
> *-Bill K.*

ity of a service provider to be vulnerable—to embrace uncommon levels of humility, selflessness, and transparency for the good of a client." Perhaps the most vulnerable we can be is to be at risk of losing the client, and yet, paradoxically, the willingness to do so (on behalf of serving the client) most often creates even greater customer loyalty.

Recently, my wife sent me to the hardware store to buy a handle that could be installed in the shower near our guest bedroom. She didn't want to screw anything into the tiles, and so my instructions were to get a handle that could be affixed with suction cups. (Do I need to point out that I'm *not* the handy one in our house?) When I explained to the salesperson what I was looking for, he refused to sell it to me. He felt strongly that using suction to potentially support the weight of a person was dangerous and an accident waiting to happen. He was willing to sell me a handle with a stronger fastening system, but not the one I came in wanting to buy. While this was an admittedly small and inexpensive issue, the salesperson was willing to risk losing my business by doing what was best for me.

Think Long-term

Here's one of the most important things I've learned about this Fundamental: Doing what's best for the client will not always work to our benefit in every individual situation. However, as an overall way of conducting business, we're rewarded many times over by stubbornly adhering to this principle. Ray Kroc, the founder of McDonald's once said, "If you work just for money, you'll never make it, but if you love what you're doing and you always put the customer first, success will be yours." If we stay grounded in always doing what's best for our client, everything else tends to take care of itself.

At RSI, this was true in all areas of our company. When a sales person focused on truly understanding and serving a prospect's needs first, we tended to make more sales. When a consultant proactively suggested a better way to solve a client's problem, even when it meant more work on our part, we built long-term loyalty. When a customer service professional went that extra mile to find a way to solve a client's problem and create a truly memorable service experience, we got more client referrals.

Remember, as well, that every one of us serves customers, be they internal ones or external ones. Put your customers' interests first and you'll build long-term relationships that are the very foundation of success. Our reputation for integrity is built upon a series of unique events in which we followed through on our most valuable commitment—to always do what's best for the client.

FUNDAMENTAL #2

Check the ego at the door.

Our own egos and personal agendas must never take precedence over doing what's best for the team. Being concerned with who gets credit, who looks good, and who looks bad is counter-productive. Making the best decision for the good of the enterprise must always be paramount.

In my observation, at the core of every dysfunctional organization is one thing: ego. When the organizational culture promotes posturing, jockeying for position, vying for credit, and political maneuvering, success is nothing more than a lucky accident. Conversely, when we submerge our egos to the overall good of the organization, when we focus our efforts and decision-making on serving others instead of ourselves, the organization will inevitably prosper and success becomes a natural result.

In discussing this Fundamental, it's important to be clear that having a strong ego is a healthy part of human development and in no way conflicts with the notion of checking the ego at the door. Having belief in yourself, your abilities, and your worth as a person are important to being successful. Checking the ego at the door is not about denying our strengths or being falsely modest. Rather, it's about making decisions for the good of the team versus making decisions to serve our ego needs.

Before I continue, let me pause here to make a subtle but important point. As I described in Fundamental #1, the foundation of any good business is in every circumstance to do what's best for the client. In fact, the organization owes its very existence to serving the clients' needs. Checking the ego at the door is about how people work effectively as a team to achieve the organization's mission—i.e., serving the client. Without effective teamwork—when egos rule—organizations become dysfunctional.

Here are some examples of behavior that would constitute checking the ego at the door.

1. Evaluating ideas on their merit rather than on whose idea it was. This sounds simple but has an amazingly powerful effect on group dynamics. Think about what happens in a typical meeting. Let's say you have six people sitting around a conference table debating the best way to approach a problem. One person puts an idea on the table. Rather than simply looking at the idea as separate from the person, we tend to tie the two together. So as the debate begins, the person whose idea it was will start to defend their suggestion because they have a personal attachment to it. Others will argue for their own points of view, hoping their idea wins so that they will look good in the eyes of others and feel good in their own mind. Each person's ego is inextricably linked to their idea and true, unencumbered intellectual debate is stifled.

Now, imagine if we all check our ego at the door and recognize that we are not our ideas. We are separate and distinct from our ideas. The idea is nothing more than an intellectual thought put on the table to be discussed, tweaked, massaged or even tossed out, and it has no bearing whatsoever on our worth. Do you see how much intellectual freedom is generated by unhooking that link between our ego and our ideas?

I witnessed this so many times at RSI, especially in management meetings. We were particularly good at checking our egos at the door. We could freely debate virtually any topic and it mattered not whose idea it was. In fact, most of the time our final decision would represent contributions from a number of people and the conclusion would be far better than any single idea that had been initially contributed.

Years ago, while working as a marketing director for a former employer, I found myself in a position of creating a campaign and pitching it for approval. The CEO's son, a Wharton School student at the time, was asked to sit in on the meeting. The student raised a question and made a suggestion that changed the focus of the entire campaign.

My first reaction was to dismiss the student's suggestion since he had little "real-world" experience and was overstepping his bounds. But then I realized I was letting my ego get in the way. I decided to check my ego at the door and really consider his point. When I did, it made a lot of sense and there was no reason not to try it. Weeks later, the campaign was a big success. I sure learned the importance of keeping an open mind and doing what's best for the team instead of what's best for my ego.
-Bill L.

2. Seeking honest feedback. Asking for feedback is a funny process. Often, what people really want is to be affirmed by hearing good comments. This is certainly natural, for who wouldn't want to hear nice things about their work? But remember, just as we are not our ideas, we're also not our work. When our ego is too tied to our work product, we're unable to hear useful feedback. Instead, we become defensive, as if someone is attacking us personally. The defensiveness causes static in our listening channel and blocks our ability to receive and process constructive feedback. When we learn to check our ego at the door, we're able to ask others for honest feedback, and we can use that feedback to continuously improve our performance.

3. Learning to ask for help rather than being a martyr. How many of us have trouble with this one? We have a big project due tomorrow and we're overwhelmed with everything that still needs to be accomplished. We're reluctant to ask for help because we're afraid we'll feel (and look) weak or incompetent; so we stay at the office until late at night trying to get it all done. Because we're tired and rushed, we make a few mistakes and the end product is not the best it could be. Notice how we let our ego needs supersede the team needs. If we check our ego at the door, then we do whatever will get the best end result. If asking for help will produce a better result for the team, then that's what we must do.

4. Being able to admit a mistake and change direction. This is one of the best indicators of checking the ego at the door. How often do we steadfastly stick to our original course, even as evidence continues to mount that it's a mistake? What keeps us from being able to simply say, "I was wrong"? It's almost as if we think that acknowledging an error makes us somehow a lesser person. I would argue, in fact, it's the opposite. The greater our confidence in our own self-worth, the easier it is for us to be free to let go of an old decision in favor of a new and better one.

Remember that the essence of checking the ego at the door is making decisions that are best for the team rather than making them to serve our ego needs. As we evaluate options, if changing from the current course will improve the probability of the team reaching its goal, then that must be our decision, regardless of anything we may have thought or said earlier.

If you'll allow me a brief diversion here, there's another fascinating dynamic that we often see at play in this whole issue of admitting mistakes and changing direction. Think about political campaigns. How often have you seen the negative campaign commercial showing the candidate ten years ago advocating for a certain position juxtaposed with the candidate today calling for the opposite? The narrator usually points to this change in view as evidence that the candidate can't be trusted. Have you ever stopped to think about how preposterous this is?

Do you have the same point of view about all topics today that you did ten years ago? I sure hope not! This is what learning, growth, and wisdom are all about. As we gain experience and knowledge, we begin to see issues from new perspectives. This new wisdom allows us to make better decisions.

I'm still waiting for the candidate who feels secure enough to check his ego at the door and proudly acknowledge that his views today are often different from those he held previously; and those in the future are likely to be different from the ones held today. This is a strength, not a weakness.

5. Making decisions that are best for the team, regardless of their personal impact. This one requires true selflessness. Sometimes the best decision for the enterprise may not be the one that's in my own personal self-interest. For example, adopting a new and improved organizational structure may mean a reduction in my responsibilities. Or choosing a different vendor might jeopardize a key personal relationship of mine. Putting team goals first gives an organization tremendous clarity and focus because there are no competing objectives. Learning to evaluate options from the perspective of organizational goals rather than personal ones is a true demonstration of checking the ego at the door.

6. Playing whatever role is required for the success of the team. We commonly hear this one discussed in terms of sports teams. The football team needs its star running back to stay in and block to provide extra protection for the quarterback, thereby diminishing the number of carries he gets. Or the track team needs a runner to sacrifice her best chance to win an individual medal by entering multiple races where team points are most needed. It's about sacrificing our own ego needs for the good of the team.

I witnessed a great example of this selflessness in our management team at RSI. We had a successful, experienced manager who had been with us for 10 years. However, as part of a restructuring of roles in order to adapt to changing market conditions, we had a greater need for him on the front lines than we did as a manager. This would mean he would now be a peer of those he had previously managed, and it would also mean the loss of his personal office. Without hesitation, he agreed to the move.

> *As the manager of our administration unit, it was my responsibility to see that our team ran as effectively as possible. At one point, I was tasked with the job of evaluating whether outsourcing one of our key services would be better than continuing to handle it in-house. This was tricky because a decision to outsource would likely mean laying off several people and would also put my own job in jeopardy.*
>
> *As I conducted my research and completed my analysis, I kept this Fundamental squarely in front of me. My job was to ensure that we could deliver high quality to our external clients while minimizing internal costs—regardless of its impact on me personally. Leaving my ego out of the equation, I ultimately did recommend and implement an outsourced solution. Putting the team goal ahead of even my career was difficult, but it was the right thing to do.*
> *-Christine A.*

Would this happen where you work? Would you be able to sacrifice your ego for the good of the team? Think about the difference in effectiveness and the greater likelihood of success in organizations where people are truly able to check their ego at the door.

FUNDAMENTAL #3

Practice A+ness as a way of life.

Regard everything you touch as a personal statement bearing your signature. Take pride in the quality of what you produce, for excellence matters as a deeply personal value in and of itself, well beyond the probable result of such excellence.

The other day, I was in the locker room at the gym where I work out and I noticed that a new sign had been posted on the glass door between the locker area and the section that houses the showers and the sauna. It was a sign asking people to keep the door closed to keep the humidity out of the locker area. The sign was sloppily hand-written and was taped to the door at an angle with Scotch tape. Now I have three questions for you:

1. What's wrong with this?
2. Does it matter?
3. If so, why?

Before we answer those questions though, let's take a closer look at this whole idea of what I call "A+ness" and see if that might cause us to view the situation through a different lens. Let's start with understanding what it is, and then turn our attention to why it's relevant.

What is A+ness?

When we were in school, an A+ was the highest grade we could achieve. An "A" meant that we had done outstanding work—top notch, but an A+ was something altogether different. It signified that we had gone above and beyond what was normally considered "excellence" and had entered the rarified air of the best of the best. It meant that we weren't satisfied with doing really well, but instead we pushed ourselves to reach further. And this is really the essence of A+ness—not being satisfied until it's the absolute best we can do.

I think of A+ness as a way of approaching life that regards what you produce as a personal reflection of who you are. It's treating everything you do as having your signature, your personal stamp of quality. And not just in the big things, but in the small details as well.

It means making sure that a document you print is accurate and neat and spaced properly on the page. It means that we don't use third generation, faded photocopies of forms, printed at an angle. It means that when we walk into a meeting, we're fully prepared and well-organized, having anticipated likely concerns and done our homework to address them. It means that the advice we give is the best and most thorough we can offer. It means that I edit and refine each of the chapters I've written in this book until I'm absolutely certain it's the best product I can generate.

Doing A+ work actually requires great discipline. So often, we reach a point in a task where we've done an adequate enough job and we simply don't feel like going the extra mile to make it even better. To be candid, I sometimes felt that way in my writing. I *did* get tired and feel like stopping short of my best. But this is where the difference lies between B+ or A work, and truly A+ achievement. Can we honestly say it's our best? Or can we dig deeper to push ourselves to do better?

At RSI, the word A+ness was used often among our people. If someone said the seminar we put on was A+, what they meant was that all the details were handled in a top-quality way. The invitations looked sharp and professional. When people arrived for the seminar, they were properly greeted and their nametags were neatly arranged on the table. The seminar started and finished on time and the speakers were of high quality. The refreshments were displayed in a way that was classy and appealing. Nothing was left to chance.

Why Is It Important?

So, why is any of this important? Does it really help us to win and keep business, and to be more successful as an organization? You may be surprised by my answer.

It's intuitively obvious that, to a certain degree, high quality is likely to generate more success than low quality is. If we're better prepared for our sales calls, we're likely to make more sales. If we do a better job serving our clients, we're likely to have better retention. If people perform their jobs more effectively, and we run our operation more efficiently, we're likely to make more money. But there's another dimension to A+ness that's important to understand.

For me, the reason to do A+ work has little to do with the result that it generates. Rather, it's because deep in our hearts we see A+ness as symbolic of the kind of person we truly are. We're the kind of person who takes tremendous pride in everything we touch. The kind of person who would do our very best even if no one else ever noticed, simply because there's no other way we can imagine approaching a task.

Some Have It and Some Don't

Here's something interesting I've found. Remember back in Institutionalizing Values when I talked about selection and I said that people generally come to the workplace with their value system largely already defined? And that there was little we were likely to be able to do to change them? Well, I've seen this to be particularly true when it comes to A+ness.

In my experience, people either have inside of them this profound pride in the quality of what they do, or they don't. And those who possess this have usually demonstrated it everywhere they've been. Whether in their church group or the PTA, coaching youth soccer or at their former employer, everywhere they go, they're about high quality. It's just who they are.

Where does this come from—this deep, abiding desire for excellence? I honestly don't know. We've all seen people from the same family who seem to exhibit widely varying degrees of it. I suspect, like many personality traits, it's partly genetic and partly environmental. Regardless of its source, we seem to either have it or we don't.

For as long as I can recall, I've always hated mediocrity. Instead, I've had this burning desire to be great; and I wanted to learn everything I could that would help me to be the best. An incident that happened in my first week of work was typical of my approach. It was May of 1983, and I had just graduated from college two days earlier. At that time, my younger sister was just finishing her first year at the University of Delaware. When my father asked me if I wanted to join him for the hour and a half drive down to pick her up, I agreed—but with one provision: that he'd spend the entire car time teaching me as much as possible about life insurance. I was hungry to be the best, and there was no time to waste.

When I think about what drove me throughout my leadership career, it was, more than anything, an overriding passion for continuous improvement. This meant trying to optimize every area. I wanted to create the best sales engine we could. I wanted us to deliver the best service possible. I wanted us to be the best management team. I wanted us to be the best at benefits administration and consulting. Every year, I would choose new initiatives that I felt were the most important ones to pursue to make us even better than we were before. I was proud of what we were accomplishing, but never satisfied, for we could always be better.

In the summer of 2004, one of my managers sent me a link to the website for the Malcolm Baldrige National Quality Award. I was immediately enthralled because here I found an entire program designed to help organizations achieve excellence in every single phase of their operation; and not just excellence, but continuous improvement. It was A+ness personified. We began to use the Baldrige model to examine and improve our own processes, ultimately becoming the only company in 2006 to win New Jersey's highest award for quality: the Governor's Award for Performance Excellence – Gold Level.

Our passion for excellence undoubtedly helped us to become more successful and make more money; but it wasn't about the money. To be clear, I'm not denigrating making more money as an appropriate motivating force for a person or a company. It just wasn't what drove me. Instead, I was inspired by A+ness; by the need to do my best. The money was a nice byproduct, but it wasn't the driving influence.

While A+ness may be the central organizing influence of *my* career, what about those who don't seem to have this inside of them? My experience is that they simply don't understand what I'm talking about. It's as if I speak another language and they cannot fully comprehend what I'm saying. They don't see anything wrong with the sloppy handwritten sign. They quite literally don't even notice it, like a person who's colorblind and can't see the number imbedded in the eye chart.

I remember when I was just starting my career; one of our very first employees was a wonderful woman whose job was to handle a variety of miscellaneous clerical tasks. Though she was good on the phone, she simply had no eye for the quality of printed documents. The fact that a document looked sloppy was totally lost on her. No matter how many times I might point out the poor spacing or the incorrect spelling, she literally could not see it. Her brain just didn't function that way. A+ness was just not a part of her composition.

I want to be perfectly clear here about something else I said in Institutionalizing Values: this doesn't mean she wasn't a great person. She was a caring, sensitive, generous, hard-working woman—who just didn't have the A+ness gene. In fact, the majority of people don't have it.

In *my* company, I wanted to surround myself with people who had this gene. People who carried inside them a tremendous sense of personal pride in everything they touched. It's one of the things I was most proud of at RSI. Though our people may have had varying skill levels and abilities, every single one of them cared deeply about doing their best. It truly *mattered* to them. I found it to be energizing, even exhilarating, to be around such a group of people every day.

So let's go back to those three questions I posed at the beginning of this chapter with regard to the sign in the locker room.

1. What's wrong with this?
2. Does it matter?
3. If so, why?

What's wrong is that the sign is sloppy and of poor quality. While the sign itself is of little importance, it *does* matter because it makes a poor statement about the gym and its attitude toward excellence. It's reflective of an organization where pride in everything you do is not a driving force.

What are *you* about and what kind of organization do you want to be associated with?

FUNDAMENTAL #4

Take the extra time to do things right the first time.

Don't take shortcuts. The goal is to get things "right," not simply to get things "done."

Several years ago, in my constant pursuit of A+ness, I was looking for a more comprehensive and refined approach to our continuous improvement efforts. As I researched the literature on the various approaches used by the best organizations, I came across the Lean Thinking movement. Pioneered by Toyota, Lean is a framework that seeks to increase the value being provided to customers while at the same time reducing cost.

At the heart of Lean Thinking is identifying the 7 key areas where we typically find "waste" and then making process improvements to reduce or eliminate this waste. One of these top 7 areas is "defects" or "rework." When we generate poor quality work, and make errors at any step in a process, we end up wasting a tremendous amount of time and resources fixing them at some later point in the process.

Just imagine the cost of a major auto safety recall. It can be devastating not only in the dollars spent but in the lost reputation as well. Every industry faces the same challenge. Think about the cost of rework in your organization and what it would mean to reduce or eliminate it. While doing quality work from the outset may take a little longer, delivering the intended value to our customer, be they internal or external, ultimately takes less time when we do it right from the beginning.

What's the Obstacle?

So, if ensuring quality upfront is so much less expensive, what keeps us from doing it right the first time? In my experience, the primary culprit is our typical definition of what it means to be productive. So often, we define productivity in terms of how many items we got "off our desk" or crossed off our list. In fact, many times our reward systems even encourage this definition by creating bonus plans tied to how many applications we processed or how many widgets we shipped. When these programs don't also contain an incentive for quality, we effectively encourage people to get things off their desk without regard for the downstream impact of poor quality. Let me give you an example that was common at RSI.

Each year, it was our responsibility to review our clients' insurance programs and make recommendations to help them manage their cost while meeting the needs of their employees. Whenever this involved changing insurance carriers, employees would need to complete new enrollment forms for submission to the new carrier. Inevitably, when we would "scrub" the forms for completeness, we'd find that a variety of information was missing—social security numbers, children's birthdates, dates of hire, and the like. And, of course, we were usually working with tight time frames in order to get the forms submitted to meet the carrier deadlines.

You can imagine the temptation to hurriedly get the forms out of our office and to the carrier regardless of their degree of completeness; for every day that they sit on our desk is a day longer that the employees may eventually have to wait to get their new insurance ID cards. But notice what happens if we succumb to this temptation to pass poor quality down the line.

The incomplete forms sit on someone's desk at the carrier longer. It's natural for them to work on the easiest things first, and incomplete forms are "messy." The carrier rep will have to call us to get the missing information, initiating a series of phone calls back and forth between the carrier, us, and the client. If the case gets processed incorrectly, some of the ID cards will inevitably be wrong, as will the first bill. These errors will prompt phone calls that will cause us to do even more work and will take still more time to get resolved.

While getting the forms "off our desk" quickly may enable us to cross something off our list, the downstream ramifications for us and for the customer are significant. If we define success as getting the job correct and complete, then rushing on the front end actually slows down the achievement of success. Interestingly, there are some insurance carriers now who have bonus programs for brokers tied to the quality of case submissions. It's actually more cost-effective for them to pay a bonus for quality than it is to spend the money on the waste and rework caused by sloppy and incomplete paperwork.

Of course, doing things "right" is not mutually exclusive with having a sense of urgency. We're all under pressure to do more with less, at lower cost, and faster. We *do* want to work quickly— as quickly as we can, but without sacrificing quality. When a conflict does exist between speed and quality, though, it's better to focus on getting things right the first time.

FUNDAMENTAL #5

Seek to create win/win solutions.

Learn to think from others' perspective. Discover what others need and find solutions that meet their needs while still fulfilling our own. Win/win solutions are always longer lasting and more satisfying than win/lose solutions.

Several years ago, my wife and I had the wonderful opportunity to work with a team of talented professionals to design and build our dream house. Central to that team was our architect. He was the one responsible for driving much of the process, from understanding our vision to creating conceptual drawings, from doing construction drawings to detailing every piece of trim, from illustrating the stonework to specifying every door knob; he was our quarterback. Though we were thrilled with his work and had been careful to discuss financial expectations upfront (see Fundamental #14 – Set and ask for expectations), we reached a point in the project where I became concerned about how rapidly our architectural fees were escalating. I decided that we needed to come up with a new arrangement, so I scheduled a meeting with him to discuss it.

As I thought about how to approach our conversation, I stayed focused on creating a win/win. From my perspective, I needed greater cost certainty and I didn't want to hesitate to call him because the meter was running. When I thought about his likely goals, I was able to come up with a suggestion that could work for both of us. Here's what we did: We agreed upon a final cost to complete the project, and I paid it to him in full right then. This gave him a fair price, helped his cash flow, and eliminated his need to bill us. It gave me the cost certainty I was looking for and eliminated my hesitancy about calling him. And to make it even more beneficial to him, I offered to work with him on a number of business issues where he wanted my advice. It was a total win/win. We both got what we wanted, we went on to finish building an amazing home, and our relationship has grown stronger and stronger over the years since.

Thinking From Others' Perspective

The operative words in this Fundamental are "seek" and "create." Win/win solutions aren't always obvious; rather, they require a certain amount of seeking and creating. They also require a degree of selflessness—a curiosity about others and their needs. It's interesting to note how many of the Fundamentals require us to go beyond our own personal perspective and learn to think from another point of view (e.g., Do what's best for the client; Check the ego at the door; Communicate to be understood; Listen generously). Seeking to create win/win solutions is an equally good example of this selflessness.

To develop a win/win, we have to put ourselves in the position of another and understand what they need. Then we can become creative about getting them what they require while also meeting our own objectives. If we can figure out a way to do both, we're highly likely to have a long lasting solution. On the other hand, if all we care about is what *we* want or need, and simply demand what we require, we often meet with resistance and, ultimately, resentment. We may achieve a "win" now, but we're likely to pay the price somewhere down the road because we've left others unsatisfied. I certainly could have demanded that my architect reduce his fee—and maybe he would have—but at what true cost? By creating a win/win instead, I kept him happy and motivated to do the best job he could possibly do.

Think about the negotiating process. If one side is determined to "beat" the other, either a deal is never struck or the one that is eventually falls apart. Here's what the prominent negotiator James C. Freund says about win/win in his book Smart Negotiating, How to Make Good Deals in the Real World:

> In a negotiation the ultimate goal is for both sides to reach a mutually satisfactory agreement. That's the only way it works; either they both "win" or there's no deal.

Sales may be the ultimate win/win game. The better we are at finding solutions to the problems our prospects face, the more business we win. In fact, it's often said that the money we make is in direct proportion to the size and the quantity of the problems we solve for others. If we're focused only on "making the sale," we tend to be less successful. When we can put ourselves in the position of our prospects, and truly understand their problems and what's necessary to solve them, then we're in the best position to succeed. We "win" the sale when we help the prospect to win.

Dealing with insurance carriers was always a good opportunity to practice creating win/win solutions. Underwriters are notorious for being conservative about approving seemingly anything. They're naturally skeptical and tend to suspect that everyone is out to "pull a fast one" on them. Understanding this, we would try to think from their perspective and try to come up with solutions that would satisfy them while still achieving what we needed. Here's a simple example.

One of our clients was up against the deadline for submitting enrollment paperwork in order to make a January 1st effective date for their new plan. The reason the deadline is so important to the carriers is that it takes them a number of weeks to do the work necessary to generate insurance ID cards, and when cases are submitted without sufficient lead time, they end up fielding calls from hundreds of frustrated employees and being blamed by the client for the mess. For this client, the January 1st date was critical, but the insurance carrier wouldn't budge on the submission deadline.

Understanding the carrier's concern, we proposed a win/win solution. We would have all the

During the past year, I've become more aggressive about finding creative ways to develop win/win relationships with my clients. When I started listening to them more carefully, it became clear that if I could help them generate more revenue for their businesses, I'd be creating a big win for them. So now I ask every client I work with about their customers and who buys their products. I put them in touch with other clients of ours, and I'm always looking for opportunities to help them in any way I can.

One of my clients is a fulfillment house, and I've put them in touch with a carrier we deal with to see if they can work together. I also have a beverage distributor that I put in touch with an entrepreneur who is looking to launch a new product in New Jersey. The distributor is intrigued with the product and is testing it now to see if it's something they can add to their portfolio.

Clients have been ultra-appreciative of my help. By learning their business and helping them grow their revenue, I've created a win/win and have set us up for a long-term, mutually beneficial relationship.

-Ralph C.

employees call our team in the ID-cardless interim, and we would field all the issues, thereby reducing the carrier's work. We would also get the client to sign a letter acknowledging the potential challenges and taking responsibility for the lateness so that the carrier would not be held accountable. This enabled the January 1st effective date to happen for the client, while still solving the carrier's problem as well. Ultimately, our solution was accepted by both.

This notion of creating win/win solutions, of course, is not just about vendors and customers. It applies to every relationship in which we're engaged. I always told our staff that I'm open to changing absolutely anything that we do at RSI in an effort to be the best we can be. However, I warned, be sure to approach every suggestion from a win/win perspective. How is this idea good for you *and* good for the company?

I remember a time when one of our employees came to me to propose a change to how his compensation program worked. He was in sales, so there was considerable flexibility about how we balanced guaranteed pay versus "at risk" pay. He created a plan that would better meet his current cash flow needs and still provide significant incentive to sell more, while at the same time guaranteeing RSI that we would recoup all of the money we were investing in him. I applauded his win/win approach and was glad to approve his plan.

Whether we're dealing with clients, vendors, employees, friends, or family, figure out a way for us both to get what we want and you'll have two parties equally committed to making it work. Think win/win.

FUNDAMENTAL #6

Practice blameless problem solving.

Treat mistakes as learning opportunities. Focus on the following questions: What are our best options to solve the problem? What have we learned that can help keep us from repeating the mistake? How will we integrate that learning into new behaviors and practices?

What's the first thing that goes through your mind when someone tells you you've made a mistake? For most of us, it's either denial or it's defense. Either we're quick to point out that we, in fact, did *not* make an error, or else we immediately launch into the litany of reasons why the error really wasn't our fault. Sometimes there's even a third response: we point out that the other person isn't perfect and we mention some of their errors. Sound familiar?

These are all quite natural responses. Obviously, none of us likes the feeling of being blamed for something, whether it truly was our responsibility or not. And unfortunately, affixing blame has practically become a national pastime. On an almost daily basis, we read articles or hear stories about outrageous lawsuits.

Whose Fault Is It Anyway?

I'm always so disappointed when I hear these stories because they all have one thing in common: the need to blame someone. If I'm walking down the sidewalk and I trip and fall, why can't we call it an "accident" and simply say that it was no one's fault? Instead, we too often look to blame the township that's responsible for the sidewalk, or the contractor who laid it, or even the civil engineer who designed the section.

Think about the disclaimers that appear on nearly every product today. What are they saying? "Don't blame me. I'm not responsible." And why are these disclaimers necessary? Because we've developed this mentality of blame. Beyond the enormous financial cost (that we all pay) for this mentality, it's tremendously unproductive.

What's the alternative? Blameless problem solving.

Blameless Problem Solving

When we practice blameless problem solving, we're first and foremost focused on solutions. A problem has occurred. The most important steps we can take immediately are to understand the various aspects of the issue, determine what options exist to solve it, choose the best course of action, and get moving on implementing the solution. Notice what's conspicuously absent in this list. Blame.

There's simply nothing useful that comes from blame. In fact, the process of determining and affixing blame actually serves to stifle the problem-solving effort. As soon as the blame starts flying, we go into our defensive posture and we're no longer thinking about solving the problem. Instead, we're consumed with all the explanations and justifications that are necessary to deflect the blame. And there's another key effect. All of that defensive "noise" keeps us from being able to learn anything from the experience.

At RSI, I always emphasized that when a mistake or problem happens, there are only three things we care about:

1. What's the best way to solve the problem?
2. What did we learn from the situation?
3. How will we reflect that learning in new processes that diminish the likelihood of that mistake happening again?

> *As I work on solving computer problems for our staff, I always keep blameless problem-solving in mind. More times than you can imagine, I look at a computer issue and realize it's been caused by a virus that attacked via a website the person had viewed. I used to get caught up in wanting to place blame, making sure the person knew that they were the cause of the issue. Of course, that would lead to finger-pointing and denial, and was a waste of time anyway.*
>
> *Now I realize the main thing is to fix the problem. Getting everyone worked up about who's at fault is mostly useless and keeps me from focusing on the solution. This Fundamental has helped me to have a totally different perspective as I approach issues; and it's made me way more effective.*
> *-Jason Y.*

Learning From Our Mistakes

How we process or "frame" mistakes has an enormous impact on how effective we are as people and, by extension, as an organization. If we see a mistake as an awful event, filled with blame, angst, and recrimination, we become so tentative that we're afraid to try new things, experiment, or extend ourselves. While this may protect our ego (see Fundamental #2 – Check the ego at the door), it certainly doesn't help us learn. Of course, for many, these are conditioned responses based on our up-bringing or our workplace environment.

A mistake is one of the world's greatest learning opportunities—if we're open to it and looking for it. Maintaining an environment where blameless problem solving is practiced allows us to keep the listening channel clear of all that defensive noise and enables us to see the important learning opportunities that are inherent in the situation at hand. These learning opportunities are important chances for us to develop our knowledge and skills.

But there's one more critical step to complete the picture. It's one thing to learn, it's another to *integrate* that learning. We must also ask ourselves how we will put this new learning into action. How will our actual behavior be *different* to reflect this learning? Problems present us with opportunities to gain wisdom. But wisdom is useful only to the extent we apply it.

Blameless Problem Solving In Action

Let me give you an example of a typical situation we would encounter at RSI, and how the various aspects of blameless problem solving play out.

As I've mentioned previously, we helped sell and service employee benefit plans for employers. As independent brokers, we represented many different insurance carriers in working with our clients and, unfortunately, there was very little standardization of forms, processes, or procedures among those carriers. One of the challenges this created was that we had to know every nuance or idiosyncrasy of each carrier we were presenting to a client. Inevitably, at some point something would get missed. It might look like this:

Let's say we're quoting prescription drug programs for a client. We show rates and benefits for six different carriers. For carriers A, B, C, D, and E, the rate we received in our proposal included oral contraceptives as a covered benefit, but in carrier F's quote it did not. We didn't pick up on this, the client chose carrier F, and the error is discovered two weeks after all the paperwork is submitted to underwriting. Now what do we do?

Well, in the typical environment full of blame, we'd spend most of our time pointing fingers. We might blame the carrier for not being clearer in their proposal, the carrier might blame us for not reading the fine print, our consulting manager might blame the consultant who presented it to the client, and the consultant might blame the administrative support person who compiled the spreadsheet. In turn, each would defend why it really wasn't their fault and deflect the blame to another. Can you see how obviously unproductive this is yet how typical it also is? Does your workplace look like this?

Now let's see how this same scenario would play out in an environment of blameless problem solving.

As soon as the problem was identified, we would immediately begin developing potential solutions. We might check to see if the carrier was willing to absorb the cost this year and build the additional cost into next year's renewal. We might see if the employer was willing to pay the additional cost. We might see if, knowing the full cost picture, a different carrier was now a better alternative and still viable. We might see if the employer was committed to having oral contraceptives included or might want to save the money and not have them covered. Once we identified all the various options, we'd determine the advantages and disadvantages of each and choose the best course of action.

After the problem is solved, it's now time to turn our attention to diagnosing what happened to see what we can learn. The diagnosis is not to figure out whose fault it was, but rather to see what learning is available. There are any number of reasons the problem may have occurred. It could be that our administrative support person didn't know to look for this issue on the proposals. It could be that we were working too quickly and didn't take the extra time necessary in proofreading our work. It could be that the carrier materials were unclear. It could be that we were not specific enough in our request to the carrier as to the benefits we wanted included.

Once we've identified the root cause of the problem, the next step is to incorporate our learning into improved processes that reduce the likelihood of repeating the same mistake. Let's assume the root cause was our lack of detail in our request for proposal (RFP). We might then implement a new RFP process that listed oral contraceptives as an option and required us to check a box indicating whether or not we wanted this benefit included. With this new procedure in place, we're much less likely to have the same problem occur again.

None of this would be possible in the typical toxic, blame-filled setting in which far too many people operate. Creating that blameless environment is what allows us to solve the problem effectively and then use the situation as an opportunity to improve our future performance.

The Future Vs. The Past

By the way, here's a simple, but amazingly powerful tip I picked up from a mentor that's related to this whole notion of our defensiveness and how it affects our ability to hear useful feedback.

When you give someone feedback for improvement, always phrase the feedback in terms of the future rather than the past. For example, suppose I needed to give you feedback about not being prepared enough for a client meeting. Notice your reaction if I say to you, "You really didn't prepare enough for that meeting and it hindered your ability to answer all of the client's questions." How do you feel? How are you likely to react? Probably with defensiveness. You'll probably try to explain the reasons why you were unable to be more prepared: you had three other meetings to prepare for; your assistant was out sick yesterday; another client threw you a last-minute curveball.

Now notice what happens if I switch from the past to the future and I say, "The next time we have a client appointment, you'll be able to handle all their questions effectively if you do some extra preparation and anticipate their needs." It's the same feedback, but you're more likely to be able to hear it and process it because it doesn't come across as blame. The past is already done. You can't go back and change it, so my harping on what you did wrong in the past isn't going to help. But the future hasn't happened yet. Helping you to see what you can do differently in the future is a much more productive conversation.

Blame is a wasteful exercise. Learn to let go of blame and watch as your effectiveness and that of those around you begins to soar.

FUNDAMENTAL #7

Make decisions that reflect a reverence for long-term relationships.

Our primary goal is the long-term success of the enterprise. We must view all of our decisions and actions from this light.

A number of years ago, we were successful in landing a very large new client. It was a case we had worked on for many months, and we were naturally excited when we heard the good news that they had selected RSI to take over managing their employee benefits. As in most cases, we had agreed to work for whatever commissions had already been built into their insurance premiums by the previous broker. And this is where the problem began.

When we notified the current insurance carrier that we had assumed responsibility for the case, we learned that only 1% was built in for commissions, as opposed to the 3-5% that was typical for a client of this size. Given the amount of work that would be involved, we were concerned about our ability to be profitable at the lower commission level, and we didn't know what to do.

Ultimately, we decided that transparency was always the best approach, so we sat down with the client to explain the situation. Our main contact, the CFO, was a relationship-oriented person and he appreciated our candor. He understood that we needed to make money, and it was important to him that we each got value from the relationship. He suggested that we mutually agree on a fair compensation and that we should bill him directly for the difference between our agreed upon compensation and the commission that had been built in. We went on to develop a fabulous relationship that benefited both the client and RSI.

The CFO I described was the embodiment of this Fundamental. While he could easily have insisted that we work for the 1% commission that was imbedded in his premiums, he recognized that the best relationships are those in which both sides prosper (see Fundamental #5). This may have cost him money in the short-term, but the long-term benefit was significant, for we were that much more motivated to deliver superior value to his company.

Heroes, Average Citizens, and Jerks

A mentor of mine, Carter Schelling, used to say that all customers fall into one of three categories: heroes, average citizens, or jerks (we renamed that last category "advantage takers!). Heroes are clients like the one I just described. They see business as a mutual relationship. They think of us as business partners. They let us get close to them because they see us as part of their team, helping them to be more successful. When there's a problem, they let us know so we can work together to solve it. They're "win/win" people.

Average citizens are clients for whom we're just another vendor. As long as we have the products and services they need at a competitive price, they continue to buy from us. They generally think it's best to keep vendors at arm's length because they believe that most people will only do what's in their own best interest. This makes it difficult to get close enough to add more value. If a competitor calls and offers them a better price, or a product they didn't realize we have, they're likely to switch suppliers without giving us the opportunity to match or beat the offering.

Jerks (or advantage takers) are those who define a successful business relationship as one in which they get more than they pay for. They're constantly trying to find ways to squeeze every penny out of us. Whether we're making money or losing money is absolutely no concern of theirs. They'll dump us in a second if they can find a better deal elsewhere. And they're always looking for that deal. Supplier relationships and vendor loyalty don't factor into how they view business should be done.

In my career, I found this to be a pretty accurate description of customer profiles. The jerks should be avoided at all costs. They tend to suck up an exorbitant amount of company time because they're never satisfied and it's ultimately a one-way relationship. Average citizens can sometimes be converted to heroes, though more often than not, they're simply "temporary clients." They help us pay the bills, and we'll hold onto them for as long as we can, though we know we'll eventually lose them. We recognize that loyalty is just not part of how they see business.

Heroes, of course, are what drive the business. They're the most satisfying clients to work with, and they're always appreciative of our efforts. In fact, their appreciation makes us that much more eager to find ways to add extra value for them. Just think about how you feel when you know your efforts are recognized. As we get to know each other better, and build more and more trust, we also become more efficient because we understand each other's expectations. There's less wasted effort. These business relationships often morph into satisfying personal ones as well.

Other Relationships

This Fundamental, though, is about more than just client relationships. It's about how we treat *all* the people we deal with on a daily basis, and about how we make decisions.

In my experience, we tend to treat people differently based upon whether or not we expect to be in a long-term relationship with them, and to some extent, this is necessary. For example, we don't take the same time to get to know the cashier at the convenience store that we rarely visit as we do a co-worker who sits in our work area five days each week. Our limited time requires that we prioritize where we invest it.

When we consider how to handle a given situation, we typically go through a similar thought process. If we expect to be in a long-term relationship with the person, we make decisions that are likely to enhance that relationship and we avoid decisions that are likely to harm it. While I'm not suggesting that we treat others poorly, I *am* suggesting that when it's likely to be a short-term relationship, we don't worry too much about how our decision will impact the relationship.

Let me give you an example. Suppose we're calling the customer service department of one of our suppliers to check on an order. The order has been delayed, and we need it to fulfill a promise we made to one of our customers. For most of us, we're likely to be a good bit more demanding and one-sided in our approach if we don't think we're likely to ever talk to this person again. All we care about is the immediate result and we're not too concerned about how our behavior might affect the relationship. However, if we know we'll have to deal with this person on many other orders in the future, we're likely to have an entirely different approach to how we get the order expedited. To be clear, I'm not suggesting that we accept a lesser result; only that we're likely to come at the problem in a different way—a way that honors the relationship.

I remember a time many years ago where it became necessary to terminate the employment of one of our staff. The members of the management team were all in agreement about the decision, but there was considerable difference of opinion with regard to the details of how the termination should be handled. Some, angry at the person being terminated, wanted to see a quick exit, certain that the sooner the person was gone, the better. Others, however, thought it important to consider how the termination would be perceived by the employee, by his coworkers, and by the clients who might be affected.

After much debate about how to proceed, we reminded ourselves that this Fundamental should govern our approach. We would handle the termination with a reverence for long-term relationships. This meant that we would ensure that the person was able to leave with his pride and dignity intact. By doing so, we were increasing the likelihood that our client transitions would be handled more smoothly and that there would be less consternation among our internal staff.

When we make decisions that honor or value relationships, we create mutually satisfying interactions. We also typically get better results. We solve problems in ways that are long-lasting rather than temporary fixes.

My son Ben is a sophomore in college. Recently, he was telling me about his budgeting for the semester. It seems that he was able to manage his spending in such a way that he has $200 more left in his bank account than he was expecting to have at the end of the semester. When I asked him what he planned to do with that money, he told me about the wonderful women who work in the cafeteria where he normally eats. Apparently Ben has developed a nice relationship with them and they always take good care of him. To show his appreciation, he decided to use his "extra" $200 to buy a $20 gift card for each of 10 workers. His heartfelt gesture of appreciation was Ben's way of thinking longer term in how he invests in relationships.

Here's what I'd like you to consider: As you go through your day, notice the various interactions you have with people and think about which ones are short-term and which are long-term. How does your approach to each differ? Where are there opportunities to make more decisions that reflect a reverence for long-term relationships? Watch what happens when you do.

FUNDAMENTAL #8

Maintain a solution orientation rather than a problem orientation.

Focusing on problems drains energy. Apply your creativity, spirit, and enthusiasm toward the development of solutions.

Recently, I was visiting my son Ben, a sophomore in college, and had the opportunity to take him out to dinner with several of his friends. It was late spring and the students had just completed registration for the fall semester, so this was fresh on their minds. As we waited for our order to arrive, I listened to the students compare notes about their experiences.

The first friend told about how frustrated he was that two of the classes he wanted to take were closed out before he could enroll in them. A second student was quick to point out that the same thing had happened to him last semester. Not to be outdone, a third friend then chimed in with his tale of woe, telling us about how he was locked out of a key class he needed and, to make matters worse, it was a core requirement for his major. For the next 20 minutes, I listened to their complaints about the unfairness of the registration process and how stupid the administration was for not fixing it.

Does this sound familiar to you? For some reason, most of us (myself included) at times love to indignantly describe how we were mistreated or wronged. In fact, the more preposterous the mistreatment, and the more justified we feel in our complaint, the more we love to share the story. But is this helpful?

After that dinner, I dropped Ben's friends off on campus, and he and I went out for dessert. As we sat outside on a beautiful April evening, we talked about the dinner conversation. In particular, we discussed how this Fundamental (yes, my kids hear about the Fundamentals too!) related to their registration experience. Ben could readily see how draining and tiresome it was to hear the complaints.

When I asked him what he could do if he got closed out of an important class, he could easily think of a number of possible options. He could talk to the professor to see if he could get an exception to be added. He could talk to his advisor to enlist her assistance. He could take another required class and see if the class he originally wanted had any cancellations once the semester began. In fact, the more Ben focused on possible solutions, the more ideas came to his mind.

We See What We're Looking For

Here's an interesting phenomenon: Have you even noticed that when you buy a new car, suddenly you begin to see that same make and model everywhere you look? Or when you learn a new word, somehow it magically begins to show up in books and magazines all around you? Ever wonder why that happens? Let me try to explain and then show you how it relates to this Fundamental.

Every moment that you're awake, your five senses are picking up signals from an infinite number of stimuli. Take just a moment right now and listen to all the different sounds that you can hear. You might hear people talking around you. And the hum of an air-conditioner or heater running. And there may be music playing. There are probably dozens of separate sounds you can pick up if you listen carefully; and the same thing is true for your other senses.

Now, if you were consciously aware of all of these different sensory inputs at the very same time, you'd probably literally go crazy. It would overload your brain's ability to process it all and it would likely overwhelm you. To protect you from this state, and to help you make sense of your world, your brain prioritizes the sensory inputs, putting some of them in the foreground and the rest in the background. For example, if you're in a conversation with someone, you pay attention to their voice and put the sound of the HVAC system in the background where you don't even notice it. This enables you to focus.

So what criteria does your brain use to prioritize the inputs and select what to put in the foreground versus the background? It prioritizes based on where you put your thoughts. Let's go back to the new Honda you just bought. There were just as many Hondas on the road around you last week as there are today. However, now that you have one, your attention is on them and your mind is moving them to the foreground, where you notice them more easily and more frequently. Whatever you put your thoughts and attention on, your mind will begin to reveal to you (even though it's really been there all along).

This is why people often say that when you make up your mind about what you're looking for, it will appear. If you put all of your thought and attention on that which you want, you begin to see pathways to make it happen that you simply hadn't even noticed before. They had merely been pushed to the background because your focus was elsewhere.

Problems or Solutions?

Now let's apply this recognition to problems and solutions. Ben's college friends were so focused on how stupid and unfair the registration process was, and on commiserating with their buddies, that they were blind to solutions that may have been right in front of them. Their brains left those in the background as it prioritized their worlds.

In contrast, Ben's thoughts and attention were on how he could get the class he wanted, not how unfair it all was. As a result, his brain allowed him to notice a variety of possible avenues he might pursue to solve the problem. It put those opportunities in the foreground where they could be seen more easily.

I'm not suggesting here that we totally ignore our problems. Sometimes it can be important and useful to focus attention on a problem to better understand its components; and as we talked about in Fundamental #6, we can often use this learning to adopt new practices that may reduce the likelihood of the problem recurring. This is quite different from simply wallowing in frustration or wasting time complaining.

What I'm really saying in this Fundamental is that we must put the bulk of our energy, our thinking ability, and our creativity into developing solutions. Remember that we'll find pretty much what we're looking for. If our attention is primarily oriented toward the problem, solutions tend to remain hidden or obscured. When we learn to focus our attention on solutions, a myriad of possibilities inevitably appears.

Be a solution-seeker, not a problem-dweller.

As an investment advisor, I work with a variety of retirement plan vendors in selling and servicing 401k plans for our clients. Often, these vendors need to communicate with the clients to gather critical data necessary for reporting. I had one vendor who constantly complained to me about how difficult a particular client of ours was to work with because they never submitted the data on time. Every time I talked to him I heard the same complaints, and the client was equally annoyed. I knew it was time to intervene.

I decided to speak straight with the vendor and help him to shift his focus to solutions instead of problems. I encouraged him to ask the client what he could do to help them gather the data, and how he might be able to make the process easier for them. Once he changed his approach, the shift in the client was immediate. It was such a simple change in orientation, but the impact was huge. Not only are the vendor and client now working well together, but this vendor has changed how he approaches his other clients as well.
-Kurt H.

FUNDAMENTAL #9

Work from the assumption that people are good, fair, and honest.

Kindness begets more kindness. Trust begets more trust. We believe that most people genuinely want to do the right thing. Act out of this belief.

If I have a favorite Fundamental, this might just be it. I think it's because this Fundamental always reminds me of the tremendous impact that our point of view has on how we treat other people and, in turn, how they react to us. A simple shift in our point of view has *enormous* potential to alter the outcome of events; and yet, so few people recognize this influence and, as a result, so many fail to seize the opportunity it presents to create success.

The Role of Filters

To fully appreciate the power of this Fundamental, we need to first take a closer look at the way in which "filters" influence our perceptions. When I use the word "filter," I'm referring to a conceptual device that alters the way in which we receive sensory data. For example, when we put on a pair of eyeglasses, the lenses alter the way in which our eyes see objects, which then alters the way our brain processes the images and how we perceive the world around us. But this notion is not limited to just our vision.

We also have filters in how we listen. While our listening filters are created in our minds and may not be physical, they have the very same role in influencing our perceptions as does a pair of eyeglasses. Let me show you a couple of examples to illustrate what I mean.

Imagine that you attend a lecture on economics presented by the head of the Economics Department at Princeton University. In the introduction, you learn that he has a PhD from Harvard, has published nine books, has been an advisor to two Presidents, and has won a Nobel Prize for his work. What influence do you think the knowledge of his credentials has on how you hear his message? Undoubtedly, your perception of his credibility is likely to cause you to believe much of what he says.

But now let's change the scenario just a bit. Suppose you see this very same man, shabbily dressed, standing on a milk crate in New York City's Central Park with a megaphone in his hand, proclaiming his theories about what's happening to our economy. The words that come from his mouth may be identical, but the way you process them and the validity you assign to them would be entirely different!

How about this one? Let's suppose that your son is a good high school baseball player, wanting to improve. Your neighbor, who's been coaching Little League for years, offers to give him some pointers about batting. How might your perception of his advice be different if you learned that he was a former major league ballplayer? Can you see the role that your filter plays in influencing how you perceive the very same information?

Here's the key point I want you to see. Once we recognize that we all have filters and acknowledge the role these filters play, we can begin to see how what we believe to be true in a situation may not be the only way of seeing it. In fact, if we choose to use a different filter, we might actually see the entire situation in a different light.

So let's look at this concept as it relates specifically to this Fundamental and our filters around trust. Let's suppose I start from the assumption that people shouldn't be trusted because they're all out to cheat me. When a check processing error is made by my bank, I call the branch and chew out the manager demanding that the problem be rectified immediately; after all, I *know* what they're trying to do to me. I'm left angry and I certainly don't win any friends at the bank. But if I work from the assumption that people are good, fair, and honest, then I assume the error was unintentional, and I calmly and politely call the manager for assistance with straightening it out. The bank responds to my courteous demeanor by quickly fixing the problem and offering my next set of checks for free as a small way of apologizing for the inconvenience. Notice how differently I see the same error and how differently I therefore respond based upon my starting assumption. Notice, as well, how people react differently to *me* depending on my assumptions about *them*.

Think about typical union negotiations. Both sides come to the table wearing glasses that have mistrust as their lenses. Since I don't trust you, I doubt the validity of your information. I question the sincerity of your offer and I look for the ulterior motive in everything you do or say. And you hear me in the very same way. How likely are we to create a win/win situation (Fundamental #5) if we look through glasses of mistrust?

Some will undoubtedly read this chapter and think I'm naïve, perhaps even foolhardy, to be so trusting. "It would be nice if we lived in a world where everyone could trust each other," they reason. "But that simply isn't the way most people are. Working from this assumption is a prescription for disaster," they'll say. I have three responses to the cynic.

Responses to the Cynic

First, I'm not suggesting that *all* people should be trusted *all* the time, even if they prove themselves to be untrustworthy. Rather, I'm talking about our starting point. If I find that every time I lend you money you fail to repay me, I'm going to stop lending you money. However, until you demonstrate otherwise, I assume you're good, fair, and honest, and I'm glad to help you out if I'm able.

Self-fulfilling Prophecy

Second, it's important to understand the self-fulfilling prophecy we create by our beliefs. There's an age-old story that illustrates this point beautifully. A wise old man is tending to his farm, which sits halfway between two towns, when a traveler happens by. When the farmer asks the man where he's going, the man replies that he's on his way to the next town and asks the farmer if he knows anything about the town. The wise farmer responds by asking the traveler what he thought of the town from which he came. "It was a terrible place," says the traveler. "People were unfriendly, they didn't like strangers, and they couldn't be trusted. In fact, that's why I'm leaving." The farmer sadly shares that unfortunately the new town is pretty much the same, and the traveler heads on his way.

Several hours later, a second traveler walks past coming from the same direction. He, too, says he's on his way to the next town and asks the farmer what he knows about it. Once again, the farmer responds by asking about his last town. This traveler, however, replies that "it was a wonderful place. Everyone was just so friendly and welcoming. Neighbors would do anything for each other and you could even leave your doors unlocked without a second thought." To this, the farmer says, "Well, I expect you'll find the next town to be pretty much the same."

My experience has shown me time and time again that you find pretty much what you expect to find. When I trust people, they tend to show themselves to be more trustworthy.

The Impact of Trust

For most of my career as a leader, we practiced Open Book Management. This meant that we taught our entire staff about the finances of the company, shared financial data, and trusted them to make good decisions. Over and over again, I saw employees treat company money as if it were their own, making smart, careful choices about spending. They responded to the trust that was given to them by demonstrating their trustworthiness.

Interestingly, I've often noticed that trusting people actually puts a tremendous burden of responsibility on them. Whenever we wrote or revised shareholder agreements at RSI, my attorney would want to meet with all the shareholders or have them seek additional counsel; but the other shareholders were never interested. They simply asked me where to sign. The complete trust they had in me was a burden I took seriously. If I knew they were going to show the documents to their own attorneys for review, I wouldn't have had to be so diligent. Instead, knowing they had given me their trust, I had to be absolutely certain I was doing what was in their best interests.

In Fundamental #1, I referred to Stephen M. R. Covey's The Speed of Trust. One of Covey's findings was that companies who've established an environment of trust realize a "trust dividend" in the form of greater speed, effectiveness, and profitability. I certainly found that to be the case at RSI. The degree of trust we had in each other allowed us to move far more quickly and successfully than most organizations.

So, the third response I have to the cynic is this: I accept that by working from the assumption that people are good, fair, and honest, I may occasionally be "burned." The alternative, however, is simply a miserable way to live. Leading a cynical life—convinced that most people can't be trusted, always on my guard—is not a prescription for happiness. Even if this viewpoint could somehow protect me from ever being taken advantage of, it would be too high a price to pay. I would much prefer to go through life treating people from a position of trust.

Becoming More Curious

There's another implication of this Fundamental that I'd like to point out. Working from the assumption that people are good, fair, and honest forces us to be more curious and to learn more about a situation before we form our judgments (see Fundamental #30). If I truly believe this person to be good, fair, and honest, but their behavior seems to suggest otherwise, then maybe I don't have the full picture. Maybe there's more to the story that I need to learn before I evaluate what I think is happening. To simply pass off their behavior as stupid or to think they must be a "jerk" is mostly intellectual laziness on my part.

It's a failure to take the time to understand how they see the world.

> One day I received an e-mail from an employee who had a reputation for being "difficult." In a previous conversation we were having, she told me how helpful she tries to be. So I tucked that in the back of my mind. When I read this e-mail, I "heard" the harsh, contemptuous tone that many people had experienced, and to be honest, I was a little annoyed. However, this Fundamental popped into my head, so I sat back and decided that I was going to re-read it, believing that she really did want to help. So I began reading...and to my amazement, I could hear her desire to help me rather than jump down my throat!
>
> This experience changed my belief about this employee and, while I haven't always heard her helpful voice at first, I try to remind myself any time I feel defensive with her that she really does mean well. And when I start from that assumption, it completely changes my perception of her and what she's telling me.
> -Sharyn S.

I remember once having a key employee who was considering leaving RSI to accept a new position with different responsibilities. Wanting to see if we could "save" him, his manager met with him to explore the possibility of redesigning his job to create a greater "win/win." We asked him to come back after the weekend with his suggestions for a better situation. The following week, he failed to do so, instead asking us to make a proposal. Hearing this news, another key manager was upset. He was sure the employee was "showing his real colors" by being unwilling to participate in a more collaborative process that would be typical of our culture. He suggested we let the person leave and move on.

Reminding everyone to work from the assumption that people are good, fair, and honest, I met with the employee to better understand his perspective. I learned that he really wanted to stay but felt uncomfortable coming up with a specific suggestion. He wanted to be clearer about how we saw him and his role and the future. He, too, had made some incorrect assumptions that were coloring his view. By assuming the best intentions, and being curious about the larger picture, I was able to explore additional options and find a way to create a true win/win outcome.

To be clear, understanding how another sees the world does not mean that I necessarily agree with them; but if I believe they're good, fair, and honest, and I understand their perspective, I'm far more likely to see a variety of pathways to our mutual success than if I simply figure they're a bad person trying to cheat me.

It's More Than Being Open-Minded

As you think about this Fundamental, I also want you to consider the difference between "working from the assumption that people are good, fair, and honest," and simply "having an open mind." Having an open mind implies a position of neutrality, or non-judgment, which generally is a good thing. However, this Fundamental asks us not to simply be neutral, but instead, to be positive in our orientation. We want to assume positive intent on the part of the other person. It's similar to the Collaborative Way practice of "listening generously" (Fundamental #18). When we start our listening by generously assuming the best intent of others, we're far more likely to generate a successful outcome. Let me give you an example.

Imagine you're one of our Employee Advocates (EAs) at RSI. You're taking over a customer from a teammate who is out on maternity leave. You've heard that this is a very difficult customer who is never satisfied no matter what you do for them. As you go to meet them for the first time, you have at least three perspectives from which you can be listening as you get to know them:

1. You can believe what you've heard and see them as difficult, never-satisfied, unfair people.
2. You can be open-minded and curious to see how they really are.
3. You can believe that they're good people who are fair, honest, and reasonable.

While many people might suggest that the 2nd approach is the best one to have, I disagree. When we follow this Fundamental and use the 3rd approach, we tend to see the good in people and we respond to them from that perspective, which most often causes them to respond in kind. And remember my point earlier: if we really do believe that most people are good, fair, and honest, then when we observe behavior that doesn't seem consistent with this, we need to suspend our judgment and be more curious to understand the situation from another's point of view. Again, this isn't simply about being foolishly nice; rather, it actually influences how other people behave. Try it and see what happens.

If your life experience has shown you that most people can't be trusted, I'd encourage you to examine what role you may have in creating this dynamic. What assumptions about people have you been operating from and how might this be affecting the outcome? Try working from the assumption that people are good, fair, and honest, and see how this changes your experience.

FUNDAMENTAL #10

Keep things fun.

The world has much larger problems than our own. Keep perspective. Be light-hearted and smile.

I was raised in a fairly traditional American Jewish family where we went to Hebrew school in addition to our regular school, went to synagogue on Saturdays, were bar-mitzvahed, and learned to celebrate the major Jewish holidays. One of the most important of these holidays was Passover. This always involved the entire family getting together and enjoying the traditional Passover Seder, with its many rituals—prayers, songs, stories, hiding the Afikomen—and a great meal. But there was another ritual that took place at those Seders, one that continues as a tradition in my family today.

You see my grandfather, at least as I remember it, was a good bit more serious about his religion than we, and presided over a Seder that was interminably long for young children like my brothers and sister and me. If you've never attended a traditional Passover Seder, you need to understand that the service takes place before you get to enjoy the meal. Antsy as we would get, my brothers and I would inevitably begin to giggle at some point, which would then lead to that panicky feeling of trying to somehow stifle uncontrollable laughter in inappropriate settings. I'm sure you know the feeling. Your face turns red, your sides hurt, your eyes tear. We would usually be sent into another room until we could calm down and "behave ourselves."

Well, to this day, every time we participate in a Seder, or for that matter, any traditional service, I flat out lose control. The minute I begin to read one of the prayers aloud, I start to laugh. While this usually gets disgusted looks from my wife and any of the more mature people in attendance, it also starts my kids and nieces and nephews laughing. I laugh so hard that my sides ache and I have to get up and walk around. Tears stream from my eyes and my nose runs. I'm literally a complete mess. And it happens every year.

Interestingly, research clearly shows that laughter is actually good for our health. It relaxes our whole body, it decreases stress hormones, and it boosts our immune system. It's even been shown to be associated with the release of endorphins, our body's natural pain reliever and feel-good drug. It's also pretty darn contagious, as my Passover tradition surely demonstrates.

So why do I share this story and what does it have to do with our Fundamentals?

Why Having Fun Is So Important

There really are three reasons I included this as one of our original core values; and, by the way, I regard it as of similar importance to the other nine. The first reason is simply that most of us spend more of our waking hours at work and with our co-workers than we do anywhere else or with anyone else. If we're going to be together that much, it sure would be nice to enjoy each others' company and to genuinely look forward to coming in to work. It's sad when I hear so many people talk about dreading work and the pit they get in their stomach every Sunday night when the weekend is coming to a close and the stress begins to build about the coming week. That surely can't be good for us.

The second reason I include this in our Fundamentals is that I believe, and my experience confirms, that we're all more productive when we're happy and relaxed. When we feel good about what we're doing and enjoy the people we do it with, we accomplish more and we produce better results. To be sure, I'm not suggesting that we never have a stressful moment, or even that we don't sometimes need some pressure to get the most out of ourselves. But we can't be successful if this is a constant state. To truly perform at our highest level, day in and day out, we need to be enjoying ourselves.

Keeping Perspective

The third reason this Fundamental is so important is one of perspective. When you genuinely care as much as we do about the quality of our work, and you're as driven as A+ people tend to be, it's easy to lose perspective. We get so caught up in trying to solve a problem for a client that we can lose the ability to step back and see where it fits in the larger scheme of our lives and the world.

I used to have to remind our people sometimes that whether or not someone received their health insurance ID card on time really wasn't a life-threatening issue. Every day we read and hear about terrible tragedies—true problems that can alter the course of people's lives. Hurricane Katrina and its aftermath was a big problem. The earthquake and the resulting tsunami in Japan was a big problem. People losing their homes—and some their lives—in the tornadoes that ripped through the South was a big problem. Children literally dying of starvation is a big problem. Not getting an ID card as quickly as you'd like is *not* a big problem.

Of course, this doesn't mean we aren't going to try our absolute best to successfully resolve the issues that comprise our daily work. Our commitment to A+ness demands nothing less of us. It's just that for 98% of us, our problems really aren't so significant. It's important for us to keep a sense of balance and perspective—and nothing helps us do that better than a good laugh.

Thankfully, we had a lot of very funny people at RSI and we loved nothing more than kidding each other and playfully teasing each other. Humorously-written e-mails and practical jokes were commonplace. And it didn't stop there.

It was not at all unusual for me to break down into a fit of uncontrollable laughter in a management meeting. Those present could always recognize the signs when it was starting to happen. I would begin to giggle about something, and it would progress from there. And once I got going, there was no stopping me (much like Passover)!

I'll always remember one particular meeting where we were including, for the first time, a new manager, Christine. I'm sure she had no idea what to expect. Our sales manager Bill, one of our funniest people, decided it would be fun to use a remote-controlled fart machine for her first meeting. He put the speaker under Christine's chair and then he'd occasionally press the button on the remote, causing a loud fart sound to come from her area. You can imagine the mortified look on her face each time it happened! Now, I'm sure some of you may think this is remarkably immature and perhaps even inappropriate. But that's the whole point of this Fundamental, isn't it? We need to be able to lighten up and not take ourselves so seriously. And there's nothing like a real belly laugh or an uncontrollable case of the giggles to cure us of that malady. I can tell you that we laughed and laughed (including Christine), and we'll all never forget it.

It's appropriate that we conclude these first ten Fundamentals—our core values—with the notion of keeping things fun. Life's quite literally too short to lose sight of the importance of having fun. Be light-hearted. Take time to smile and laugh. And if your laughter becomes contagious and uncontrollable, and your sides ache, all the better.

SECTION 2

Focus on Service – These habits help to create extraordinary service experiences.

Fundamentals 11 through 17 all describe practices that are primarily focused on how we work with others: customers, suppliers, and each other. I've always believed that we're all in a customer service function. Some of those customers are external, while others are internal; but we're all serving someone.

At RSI, we wanted to create the type of service experiences that would make people remember them and talk about them. We wanted them to be truly extraordinary, i.e., beyond the normal expectations. Practicing these Fundamentals was instrumental in achieving that goal.

FUNDAMENTAL #11

Create a feeling of warmth and friendliness in every client interaction.

Every time you touch a client you're on stage. This includes calls, visits, voicemail, letters, e-mails, and other communications. Make dealing with you an extraordinary and memorable experience.

The other day, I was sitting in a restaurant trying to choose what I wanted when I noticed the line at the bottom of the menu that said, in bold letters, "ABSOLUTELY NO SUBSTITUTIONS." This was after I hung my coat on a hook by which a sign announced, "We are not responsible for lost or stolen items." What kind of feeling do you get when you read signs like these? They certainly don't make you feel welcomed. Whether we recognize it or not, we're sending messages to our prospects and customers in every interaction we have.

I've always felt that there are two components to every client interaction. The first, I call the "facts" or the "details" of what takes place. This includes whether or not we solved the problem, whether we communicated in a clear way, whether we answered the question at hand. The second component is what I call the "experience." On a more emotional level, what was it like to deal with us?

We're creating an experience, whether intentional or not, every time we interact with a client. Most of us recognize obvious examples of this—a customer service phone call, a site visit, or a client meeting. But remember that even our written communication creates a "touch point" with clients as they read it, and this creates an experience. In the moment they're reading our letter, e-mail, note, or fax, they're sharing an experience with us.

There are a myriad of different ways in which we interact with clients, and in each one we have a unique opportunity to create an extraordinary experience. We're limited only by our awareness and our creativity. Let's take a look at some of those interactions.

1. Face-to-face. The most obvious customer interaction is when we're meeting someone in person. No doubt you can think of times when you walked into a store or a restaurant or any other business and you were greeted by a genuinely friendly person with a big smile on their face. They made you feel good about doing business with them. Undoubtedly, you can also think of many times in which you experienced just the opposite. When the person greeting you had a sour expression and gave off the feeling that they were doing you a favor by serving you, versus the other way around. Even their posture sent a message of either friendliness or disinterest.

Pay particular attention to the first person who greets a customer, for they set the initial tone for the entire customer experience. Whether this person is a receptionist, a hostess, a greeter, a ticket agent, or even a salesperson, they play a critical role in setting you up for success.

Think about the language we use and how it contributes to creating a feeling. I'm always amazed when I say "thank you" to a cashier after completing a purchase and they respond with, "No problem." No problem? As if giving them my business might be a problem, but they're willing to overlook it? A more appropriate response might be, "No. Thank *you*. We really appreciate you shopping with us today and hope you'll come back soon."

2. Over the phone. For many businesses, the primary means of interacting with customers is over the phone. A couple of years ago, we switched our auto insurance to a new carrier. Since that time, I've been nothing but impressed with the friendliness and helpfulness they convey in every conversation. There's a genuine warmth that comes across on the phone. They seem eager to help, like they appreciate my business and enjoy the opportunity to work with me.

On the other end of the spectrum, I recently ordered a pair of shoes from a business I found on the web. After the phone rang six or seven times, a gruff voice answered in such a way that I wasn't sure if I had even called the right number. Eventually, I was passed to someone who could take my order, and I felt like they thought they were doing me a favor. Needless to say, I won't do business with them again.

3. In writing. This is a place that's often overlooked when we think about client interactions. When we send a letter or an invoice, or even a packing slip, we're interacting with a customer. What feelings do we convey by our choice of words? Is our letter officious and unfriendly? Or does it make the reader feel comfortable and appreciated?

I've always tried to remind our people that in everything we write there's a tone or a mood that's created between the lines. We do this through our word selection, through our sentence structure, and even through the size of our paragraphs. For example, compare the feeling conveyed by these two passages:

a. It has been brought to our attention that the aforementioned purchaser has failed to fully comply with the terms of our purchase agreement thereby nullifying any right to a refund.

b. I'm sorry. It seems as though we may not be able to refund your money because you've already used the product you bought. However, if we're mistaken, or if there's more to the story than we realized, please call us so that we can be sure you're treated fairly.

Notice the difference in tone. The second passage obviously creates an entirely different perception.

Before you hit the "send" button on your e-mail, read it carefully, not only for correctness (see Fundamental #26), but also for its underlying tone. Something as simple as putting words in all caps can make it feel like you're yelling at your reader, a distinctly unfriendly feeling—and one that may be unintentional. Look for opportunities to "warm up" your writing.

Recently, I ordered a home ultrasound unit to help me in rehabbing a hamstring injury. I've been quite impressed with the tone of all the company's communications, including their website, their order confirmation, the instructions that came with the unit, and the follow-up e-mail I received. Following is the text of the e-mail that came a week after getting the unit.

This is Paul from the MendMeShop.com following up. You recently made a purchase from our online store. We are the company that sells the home Ultrasound device, the Inferno line of Wraps, and the Freezie Cold compression wraps.

I noticed that you've had your products for awhile now - this is just a courtesy email to see how you are getting along with your treatments. I am here to help with any questions you might have about regarding how to best use the products, your injury/condition, or anything else that comes to mind.

After all, it is in every one's interest to ensure you have the best possible information in helping you to overcome your injury or condition. We have been in business almost 5 years now and we will continue to be here to help you every step of the way.

Anytime questions or concerns arise, let me know via email or call me toll free at 1-866-989-6431. Myself, or one of my colleagues, will do our best to help.

While I might have changed a few words here and there, it's the style I'd like you to notice. The overall tone of the e-mail conveys a genuine interest in making sure that I'm getting what I paid for. It certainly makes me more likely to do business with them again.

And if we want to take our warmth and friendliness up another notch, consider this example. My wife recently ordered a pair of shoes from the company Zappos. Here's the e-mail she received confirming the order:

Hello Catherine!

Your order with Zappos.com has shipped. YAY! We've enclosed some tracking information, so you can follow your order to its final destination. It's almost like being a superspy! Mission Control advises that you take a look at the top-secret information below.

Right after that, she received the following e-mail regarding the shipping:

> Whoa, Nellie! Have We Got A Surprise For You!
>
> Hello Catherine!
>
> Although you originally ordered Standard Shipping, we're upgrading the shipping time frame for your order. It will ship out today, so you'll get it even faster than we originally promised! It's kind of like we waved our magic wand!
>
> Please note that this is being done at no additional cost to you. It's our way of saying thanks for being our customer.

What a refreshing change from the usual drivel we see! Granted, they're selling a fun product and not legal services, but I think you can see that there are unlimited opportunities to warm up what would otherwise be dry and impersonal communications. By the way, Zappos has done a fabulous job of defining their culture through 10 core values, one of which is "Create Fun and a Little Weirdness." Each of their values is explained fully, in plain English, on their website. It's worth checking out at http://about.zappos.com/our-unique-culture/zappos-core-values.

Here's a simple tip about an often misunderstood rule: Use contractions whenever possible. While many of us have been taught that business writing should be formal, I disagree. Which gives a friendlier feel? "I am sure you will enjoy your stay" or "I'm sure you'll enjoy your stay." The e-mail from MendMeShop.com could have been helped by using more contractions. Contractions have an informality to them that makes us feel more relaxed and more comfortable. Don't be afraid to use them.

4. One-way communications. Be aware that you're creating a feeling even in your "one-way" communications. Your voicemail greeting creates a sense of your style and sets an expectation for callers (see Fundamental #15). It should leave callers eagerly looking forward to talking with such a friendly person. What impression does yours create for those who call you?

The signs and notices we post are another form of one-way communication, and they definitely create a feeling. The signs I referred to in the first paragraph of this chapter are a type of customer interaction, albeit a distinctly negative one. Every sign you see can easily be made more friendly. Instead of saying "All forms MUST be completed in full," we can say, "We appreciate your help in completing the forms to the best of your ability. If you need further help, please just ask us." Which business would you rather deal with?

A number of years ago, our corporate attorney advised us that it was important to put a confidentiality disclaimer on the bottom of our faxes and e-mails. You know the ones I'm talking about—they're usually ten lines of legal language that sound very intimidating. I was terribly uncomfortable with this, as it ran totally counter to everything we stood for in our communication style. Ultimately, I wrote my own, friendlier version that was a reasonable compromise. Here's what it said:

> While we at RSI take seriously our responsibility to communicate in ways that are simple, clear, and accurate, mistakes do occasionally happen. If you've received this confidential message in error, please delete it from your system and let us know so that we can correct the problem and get the message to the right person. Thank you for your understanding.

This certainly has a different feel than the typical disclaimer. Be aware of the tone you're creating in *every* area of your communications, and make sure it's as friendly as possible.

Be Easy to Work With

In addition to these various forms of interacting with customers, we also send a message by how easy we make it to work with us. Recently, I found myself needing to change a flight due to a snowstorm, but the airline charged me a $150 change fee. When I called to ask this to be refunded, I was told that I had to send an e-mail to customer service to make this request. My e-mail then generated an automated response e-mail letting me know that the current response time was 7–9 business days. When I hadn't heard anything in nearly three weeks, I tried calling the reservations line again. I was told there was no phone number for customer service and that I would have to write another e-mail. Incredulous, I searched all over their website looking for a phone number. Sure enough, there is absolutely no way to call customer service to discuss the issue. It can only be done by sending in a request and waiting for a response! As I tried to work through the issue, I found myself getting angrier and angrier. Rather than creating an easy, friendly experience, they made it amazingly difficult to work with them.

When I call your business, do I have to go through 17 prompts to eventually find my way to someone who can help? Is there an easy way for me to bounce out of the system if I want to talk to a live person? Think how frustrated you get when caught in voicemail mazes, and understand what this does to your customers.

I had the complete opposite experience while working with Amazon. I recently had a problem with the power cord to my Kindle. When I went to the website to look for customer service contacts, I found that I could simply put in my phone number and they would instantly call *me*! I spoke with a friendly person who happily shipped a new cord to me at no cost. I like buying from Amazon. They're always easy to do business with and they make me feel appreciated. Every interaction carries a tone of warmth and friendliness.

Here's perhaps the most amazing thing about being friendly: it's free! It doesn't cost one penny more to smile at someone and be nice than it does to frown. It's no more expensive to write a letter using friendly words than it is to be formal and standoffish. It doesn't take a bigger budget to have the signs we post show our customers that we value them. All it takes is awareness and intention.

When people deal with us, they don't necessarily know or care about our reputation, our culture, our strategy, or our values. The only thing that's "real" for them is the current experience they have with us. Amaze them with your helpfulness. Surprise them with your friendliness. Delight them with your warmth. Cause them to look forward to their next opportunity to connect with you. Make the experience one that prompts them to tell stories about how wonderfully they were treated.

FUNDAMENTAL #12

Practice the "Human Touch."

Treat people as individuals and show them you care. Look for opportunities to acknowledge their uniqueness and their human-ness (calls, cards, notes, gifts, etc.).

Recently, I was returning home from a family vacation in the Caribbean during my children's spring break. Our flight was connecting through Charlotte, where we had to clear customs before continuing on to Philadelphia. As is typical in airports, we were herded like sheep from one place to another until we reached the line for customs. Though there were probably ten or twelve stations, I noticed that the travelers immediately in front of us at our station seemed to be laughing and joking with the customs agent, unlike those in all the other lines. I was curious to see what was going on as it became our turn to step forward.

Sure enough, the agent had a wry smile on his face and a twinkle in his eye. I could tell he was planning to joke with my daughter. He asked her name, what she had been doing, the names of the rest of her family, and what her father did for work. Noticing her college sweatshirt, he jokingly asked if she went to another college. When my daughter began to blush, he couldn't help but tease her (in a friendly way). After a few jokes aimed my way, he wished us a great day and got ready to greet the next traveler. It certainly was not what we expected from the typically stoic customs folks.

At the heart of every great customer service story is the experience of being treated as an individual. Each one of us wants to be recognized for our uniqueness, for our personal value. Unfortunately, in most of our dealings we feel "processed," like an inanimate object in a transaction. Just think of how we're treated on most flights—from the way we check our bags, to the way we go through security, to the way we board, to the way we're given safety instructions. Even when the flight attendant uses friendly words to welcome us to the new city and remind us "to be careful because items may have shifted in flight," it feels automated or canned. Rarely do we feel truly cared for as an individual— and yet this is what we all crave.

So what keeps us from treating people as individuals, and what can we do to change this? Let's take a closer look.

Why We Don't Practice the Human Touch

I think there are three primary reasons why we so often fail to practice what I call the "human touch" in our business interactions. The first is that we frequently define, and therefore teach, business processes in terms of the transaction instead of the human connection. For example, when most stores teach a new cashier their job, they define the job as accurately completing the purchase transaction. As a result, they focus the training on teaching the employee how to scan an item, how to press the right buttons on the register, how to handle a credit card or a check, and what to do if there's a problem. While these are all important, I contend that the real job is to create a positive purchasing experience for the customer. If we defined it this way, we'd put more of our focus on how we greet the customer, on making eye contact, on smiling, on making personal conversation. While this certainly happens on occasion, it's usually the fortunate result of a person with a permanently happy disposition, rather than it being a consistent, predictable way of dealing with customers. No doubt this was the case with my customs agent. He was determined to be happy and create a positive experience, *in spite of* what he had probably been taught, not *because of* it.

The second reason we so often miss the chance to create a more human connection is that we've created an orientation toward what we think is efficiency. We've built systems and processes designed to handle as many people in as little time and at as little cost as possible. We create automated voice response units so that callers never have to talk to a person. We can now make purchases, sign up for events,

> *As one of my clients was going through Open Enrollment, they were changing carriers and plans, so every employee had to complete a new application and additional paperwork for the year. One of their employees just had back surgery and would not be able to get into the office to fill out the forms. I could tell the employee was getting nervous and upset, especially due to her current medical condition, and she didn't want to risk losing coverage. I needed to help so she could relax and not jeopardize her health.*
>
> *I asked her if it would be OK if I came to her home to visit and bring all the necessary paperwork. She was quite surprised that I would "go out of my way" to help her! We had a great visit and we were able to get everything completed and submitted to the carrier. I called her a few weeks later to see how she was doing, and she was happy to report all was going well, both physically and with her benefits. A few months later, I was attending one of the client's Health Fairs and saw her, and it felt like I was running into an old friend.*
> *-Linda K.*

order tickets, find out our mortgage balance, and perform any host of other activities without needing to interact with a human. Even when people are necessary, we create standard procedures (think of the airlines) so that we can handle a large volume of activity more easily. Everything is geared toward treating everyone the same, following the rules, and making no exceptions. To be sure, not all of this is bad. It's just that we've been so focused on how to increase our efficiency, that we've given scant thought to how to effectively create more human experiences. However, as I'll show you, there *are* ways to combine the two.

The final reason I believe we don't usually create human connections is that most of us tend to be self-absorbed. I don't mean that in a harsh way. I simply mean that we're so absorbed in thinking about our own lives, and the things we need to get done, and the pressure we're under, that we rarely take time to really notice and pay attention to the uniqueness of those around us. Noticing other people requires us to be paying attention to something other than ourselves.

Fortunately, we have an infinite number of ways that we can combat this tendency. Let's begin by looking at two great examples of using a process approach to actually *increase* individualization.

Using Process to Drive Individualization

In the first two chapters, I wrote about Ritz-Carlton and their extraordinary service. One of the practices they emphasize is noticing and recording guest preferences. They use specially designed pads to record any guest preference they notice—from how you like your coffee, to which newspaper you'd prefer, to what type of room you like. Everyone is empowered to note and record these observations. The preferences are then entered into their computer system. When a frequent guest is returning to the property, their name and preferences are reviewed in the Daily Lineup. In this way, everyone is tuned into creating a truly personal experience.

Here's another example of noticing and recording personal information. Years ago, I read Harvey Mackay's great bestseller, <u>Swim With the Sharks Without Being Eaten Alive</u>. In it, he describes a customer profile he calls the Mackay 66. It's a form he uses to record a plethora of information about each customer. It includes their birthday, the names of their spouse and children, where they went to school, their hobbies, their other professional contacts, their favorite teams, whether or not they drink or smoke, their religious affiliation, and on and on. If we're trying to complete as much of the profile as possible, we have to be paying attention to the customer and what makes them unique. And when we're paying attention, we notice opportunities to treat them with the "human touch."

I spent 8 years at RSI before I went on to start my own small business. One of the many Fundamentals I practice every day is the Human Touch. It's important in my business to create very personal relationships with my clients. I've learned to listen closely for the details of their personal stories and to record them in my notes.

Recently, I was talking with a client and could tell she was upset. When I asked, she shared that her dog had just been diagnosed with cancer. Knowing how devastating this was to her, I followed up with a personal note to let her know I was thinking of her. Several days later, she left me a message letting me know how much that gesture touched her. I really do care and I try to look for personal ways to show people I'm thinking of them.
-Maureen W.

The best way for me to show you that I value you as an individual is to listen for and recognize your uniqueness. Let me give you plenty of examples of how this can be done:

- If I know where you went to school and I read an interesting article about that school, I might cut it out and send it to you with a personal note.

- If I know that your daughter plays lacrosse, I might call you after an important game to see how it went.

- If I know your birthday or anniversary, I might send a *handwritten* card or call you on that day.

- If I know you're in the process of helping your child decide on colleges, I might share a useful article I saw, call you to find out their choice, or even connect you to someone I know who attends one of your child's top choices.

- If I know your father is ill, I might send a *handwritten* note letting you know I'm thinking of you.

- If I know you've been planning on running your first marathon, I might call to check in on how your training is going.

- If I know your favorite author, I might let you know that I saw he's just published a new book, and perhaps I might even have a copy sent to you.

I think you get the idea. Notice that all of the examples listed above involve little to no cost. People don't need you to buy them gifts and take them to ballgames. In fact, in some environments these may be prohibited or severely limited. What people want is to be noticed and acknowledged for their uniqueness.

The Value of Handwritten Notes

In the examples I provided, you may have also noticed that I italicized the word *"handwritten."* There are few things that scream "personal" more than handwritten notes. The very fact that you wrote it out tells the recipient that, at least for the few minutes it took you to compose the note, you were thinking specifically about them. On the contrary, receiving a printed note where my name has been inserted by a mail-merge computer program does *not* make me feel unique.

Here's one of my pet peeves: getting holiday cards with no written note included. Of all the cards you get, how many have nothing but a stamped company name in them? Few things make me feel more "processed" than receiving cards like these. Having my name on the list to get the auto-generated holiday greeting most assuredly does not make me feel special. I would much rather not get a card at all. The company sending them is actually wasting money and creating ill will!

By the way, sending cards with just a signature is nearly as bad. Once again, it suggests that you completed the assembly line process of signing your name to all the cards without ever thinking of me as an individual. At RSI, we did send birthday cards and holiday cards. However, I required that all cards must have a handwritten note in them. If you don't know the person well enough to say something to them, then you shouldn't be signing the card in the first place. It comes across as not being genuine.

I made extensive use of handwritten notes for all types of occasions. As I mentioned in Institutionalizing Values, I wrote personal welcome notes to all new employees. Whenever possible, I tried to include something unique about the employee that I learned from the hiring manager. Sometimes I'd write a note just to let someone know I noticed what they were doing and appreciated their work. Other times, I'd write a note to thank them for some particular contribution.

One of the most powerful examples of the impact of personal notes was when I distributed bonus checks. At the end of each year, we would distribute a share of our profit to all employees according to the rules of our Open Book Management program. Every year, in addition to the check, I would handwrite a note to each employee, acknowledging something specific about their contribution. With approximately 100 people, this was an exhausting effort. It required me to really think about each person individually, and I usually wrote a paragraph or two for each. Many people would tell me that these notes meant more to them than the money; and to this day, many tell me that they've saved every one of those notes I wrote over the years.

> *One day, I was speaking to an employee who needed to terminate her son from her insurance coverage because he had enlisted in the military. During the call, she shared her fears about him being deployed to Iraq. We talked for a while about the commitment and maturity it takes to enlist, knowing you'll be deployed to a hot spot. I shared that my family is a military family and how thankful we are to those who volunteer for service.*
>
> *I noted her son's deployment date on my calendar. After he left the States, I sent his mother a note of encouragement and promised to keep her son in my prayers until his return. When she received the card, she called me, her voice catching with emotion because she was so touched that I really heard what she was going through—so much more than just removing a dependent from her insurance plan. Fifteen months later, I was pleased to hear that her son had returned home safely.*
> *-Nora M.*

Live Receptionist Vs. Automated Systems

Here's yet another way of showing the "human touch." How many businesses still have a live receptionist answering the phone?

Because we recognized the important role the receptionist often plays in setting the tone for a customer interaction (see Fundamental #11), we made it a priority to always greet callers with a warm and friendly person. While this became more and more difficult as the volume of calls increased, for us it represented a commitment to creating that human touch. We even went to using two receptionists to maintain this approach. Certainly we could have saved money by using an automated answering system to direct calls, but it ran counter to everything we stood for.

In a world that's become increasingly depersonalized, we can make our companies stand out as the exception. Look for every chance you can to show people that you really do care. Remember people's names. Take note of and remember their interests, their family situation, their concerns. Send them personal, handwritten notes. Send them a book or a gift that you know will be meaningful. Call them at home in the evening to check on their health if you know they needed care. Be a friendly person they can connect with on a human level. Make dealing with you a pleasant reprieve from the normal experiences people have with most of their vendors.

There is no substitute for being genuine.

FUNDAMENTAL #13

Communicate to be understood.

Know your audience. Write and speak in a way that they can understand. Use the simplest possible explanation.

Here's a simple question: What's the purpose of communication? I think it's for two (or more) people to understand each other. So if I'm writing or speaking, the barometer of success is equally simple: Did the other person clearly understand what I intended to communicate?

Have you ever read a letter from an attorney and had no clue what half of it meant? Or shopped for a computer and felt like you only understood a fraction of what the salesperson told you, as if he was speaking another language? How about sitting through a presentation where the speaker constantly referred to industry terms for which you were sure you were the only one who didn't know the meaning? How did these experiences make you feel?

Most of us feel uncomfortable, embarrassed, and even ignorant when placed in these situations, as if we're somehow lacking because we can't understand what the other person is trying to get across to us. Using my barometer for effectiveness, I'd call these attempts at communication failures; and I'd put the responsibility for that squarely on the shoulders of the author, salesperson, or speaker.

If the purpose of communication is for people to understand each other, then why do writers and speakers so often choose to use complicated words when simpler ones will do, or insist on using language that's particular to their own industry, or sometimes even their own company? Sadly, I believe the answer is selfishness—a focus on ourselves and our own agenda versus the audience and their needs. Communicating to be understood begins with shifting that focus *away* from ourselves and *to* our audience.

Here are some guidelines for communicating in a way that others can understand:

1. Know your audience. This is probably the most important rule. If your goal is for your audience to understand you, then you need to choose words and descriptions that will make sense to them. If I'm a computer whiz, I need to use entirely different language speaking to a convention of network administrators than I do speaking to someone who barely knows how to turn their computer on. If I'm an attorney, I need to write differently arguing a brief for a judge than I do sending a letter to a client. It's not about me and my ability to impress people; rather, I need to check my ego at the door (remember Fundamental #2) and focus on the needs of my audience.

2. Don't use industry (or internal) jargon. Every industry has its unique language—words with which others in your industry are completely familiar, but those outside your industry don't know. And every company has its own set of acronyms, abbreviations, and internal code speak that's foreign to outsiders. When we're absorbed in our own world, we forget that everyone else doesn't necessarily speak our language. Get into the world of your audience and speak their language.

3. Define your terms. Sometimes it's simply too cumbersome to explain everything without using any industry terms at all. In these cases, it's entirely acceptable to use those terms, provided you define them for your audience first. Let me give you an example.

My company would frequently lead open enrollment meetings for employers where we would be responsible for explaining the employee benefit offerings to their employees. The audience would be composed of every type of employee at every educational level. You can imagine that the insurance industry has a language all its own, and it's one that tends to intimidate many people.

It can be difficult to explain how a plan works without using a single insurance term, so it's often necessary to use some terms, but only after defining them. I might say something like, "In this plan, you choose a doctor who will be the one to coordinate all of your care. We call this person a Primary Care Physician, or sometimes a PCP." From here forward, it's OK for me to use the term "PCP" because I've explained what it means. Try to avoid using industry- or company-specific language, but if you must, be aware that you're doing so and define the terms first.

4. Use the simplest possible language. If two different words or phrases will work equally well, use the simpler one. In our industry, I used to hear insurance carrier reps talk to employee groups about what you have to do when you need to "access care." Now I don't know about you, but I never "access care." I go to the doctor! Big words aren't necessarily more impressive or effective. Speak (and write) simply and plainly.

A great example of this practice is the "…For Dummies" series. While I don't particularly like the inference that anyone who doesn't understand technical information is a "dummy," the books are beautifully done. They've tapped into this whole recognition that we ought to be able to explain almost anything in simple terms that anyone can understand, and they're tremendously effective at doing it.

> *Recently I was asked to meet with an organization wanting to put a new 401k plan in place. It's very common for new companies to want this kind of retirement plan, but there are many pitfalls they need to be aware of prior to doing so. The biggest obstacle is typically the discrimination testing required on 401k plans, and the rules can be somewhat complex. I knew that in going through this, I could easily get caught up in all the industry jargon (ADP/ACP tests, HCEs, NHCE, etc.).*
>
> *As I prepared to meet with the executive team, I thought about this Fundamental and the importance of keeping my explanation as simple as possible. By using plain English and avoiding all the technical terms, I was able to help the team understand the essence of the rules and what we needed to do to ensure success. In the end, we were able to put a plan in place that met the needs of both the organization and the staff.*
> *-Nate T.*

5. When writing, use short paragraphs, subtitles, and bullet points whenever possible. Have you ever noticed how intimidating long paragraphs can be? Long paragraphs often look too complicated and include too much information. Break what you want to say into smaller, bite-size chunks that are easier for your reader to grasp. Subtitles also serve to separate and announce ideas so that your reader can digest them more easily. Notice how I've tried to use both of these suggestions throughout this book.

Another way to make information easier to understand is to use bullet-pointed lists. Often, I can more quickly grasp your main ideas if you give them to me in a list than if I have to glean them from several long paragraphs of text.

6. Use a Q&A format whenever possible. One of the most effective ways to get a large body of information across is to create a Q&A format. This enables you to identify the key questions your audience is likely to have, and to answer them in a clear and concise way. More and more, we're beginning to see companies publish Frequently Asked Questions (FAQs) in owners' manuals, on websites, and in other documentation. Where appropriate, it's helpful to break these questions into groupings by topic. This makes it even easier for the reader to quickly find the information he's looking for.

7. Provide your audience with a filing system. Imagine that you're my new executive assistant, and one of your

In my role as a compliance consultant, one of my primary jobs is taking complex, technical concepts and explaining them to our clients in a way that they can easily understand. I do this partly by using simple language, but I also do it by how I organize the information I want to convey.

In 2008, the Department of Labor (DOL) issued revised final regulations for the Family Medical Leave Act (FMLA). It was 201 pages of mostly unnecessary verbiage; and my team's task was to summarize it in a way that was useful for our clients. We organized the material into 16 topic-specific sections, each having a plain English summary, real life examples, and specific action steps for compliance—and we did it all in 9 pages!

It felt good when one of our clients told us that it was the most helpful FMLA summary they had received from any source, including their law firm, their HR association, and other consulting firms. That was exactly the feedback we were aiming for!
-Kara B.

jobs is to file away all of my papers so that I can easily access them when I need them. No system exists yet, and on your first day I dump a stack of hundreds of various unlabeled papers on your desk with instructions to get them filed by the end of the day. How effective are you likely to be?

I think of my audience in the same way. I'm going to be feeding you bits of information as I speak. As you listen, your brain is trying to organize the various bits of information and determine how they relate to each other and where to put them. If you have no idea where I'm going, this is terribly difficult to do. However, if I first explain to you what I'll be covering, in what order, and how the pieces will ultimately come together, then you'll know how to "file" what I'm giving you as I progress through the talk.

In a book, typically the Introduction and the Table of Contents together become the filing system. They tell you what to expect and help you to see how each piece fits into the whole. With this in mind, it's easier to understand the material you're reading.

Notice the common denominator in all of my guidelines? They're all about serving your audience. And after all, isn't that the purpose of communication?

When I was in sales, I was successful for one primary reason—people *trusted* me. And what built that trust more quickly than anything else was my ability to explain insurance to people in a way that was unintimidating and easy to understand. Think about how we feel when people speak "over our head." Because we don't completely comprehend what they're saying, we often don't trust them. At the very least, we're uncomfortable and prefer not to do business with them. But when we can easily understand them, especially when the topic is complex, we feel as if we're in good hands.

I always told our people that one of the greatest compliments you can get is when a prospect or client says to you, "Wow. I never understood it so clearly before!" That's when you know you were able to communicate to be understood.

FUNDAMENTAL #14

Set and ask for expectations.

We judge situations not by what happens, but by how they compare to what we expected to happen. Learn to create mutually understood expectations in every situation.

We judge situations not by what happens, but by how they compare to what we *expected* to happen. It sounds pretty simple, doesn't it? But as we take a closer look, you'll see just how big a statement it really is and why it's a cornerstone of both business and personal relationships.

Let me give you an example I often used to teach this concept to new employees at RSI. Imagine that you were a new employee coming to work for RSI and I told you at the end of the first day that one of our customs was to give each employee a check for $500 on their second morning of employment. It's just our way of saying, "We're glad to have you on board and we have confidence that you're going to be a great contributor to our organization." No doubt you'd be pretty excited and all the more certain you'd made the right choice in coming to work for us.

So now it's your second morning and on your desk when you arrive is a check for $200. You'd likely be a little disappointed. You might wonder if you'd done something wrong, or if perhaps we didn't have as much confidence in you. See, your expectation was that you'd be getting $500 and you only got $200.

Now let's try this scenario differently. Let's suppose I said nothing to you about our custom. You come in on your second day and there's a check on your desk for the very same $200. What's your reaction? You probably think you work for an amazing company (and can't wait to see what happens on the third day!).

Interestingly, the amount of money is identical in both scenarios. Yet the reaction is entirely different. So the real issue, clearly, is not the amount of the money. Rather, the issue is how reality compared to what you were expecting.

It's my observation that we have expectations for every future event. Sometimes those expectations are conscious and easily identified. We can describe them to one another. Other times, we're not as aware of our own expectations. We've never given them much thought, yet we do have expectations for everything. You have expectations for what you thought this book would be like. You have expectations for how your day at work will go. You have expectations for how a colleague will react to a message you give him. You have expectations for how your lunch will taste. You have expectations for how long a meeting will last. You literally have expectations for everything.

More importantly, your reaction to today's events will be directly related to how they compare to the expectations you had for the event—whether conscious or not. Why is this so important? Because this essential, yet obvious, principle has enormous implications for not only every service business, but for every interpersonal interaction as well.

Let's look at a typical example that happens every day in almost any business. A customer calls you on Monday morning and asks you to check on the status of their order. You promise to look into it and get back to them. The next day, proud of yourself for your responsiveness, you call with the answer. Yet the customer is unhappy that it took you so long to get back to them. They were expecting an answer the same day. Now, suppose they weren't expecting an answer until Wednesday. You're a hero because you responded by Tuesday and beat their expectation.

Here's the critical point to understand: If the customer is going to judge you by how your response time compares to their expectation, what could possibly be more important than finding out exactly what they're expecting? And yet we still frequently get off the phone without having established a clear expectation.

> *Recently, I had a situation that really showed me how important it is to ask for expectations. I had a client who was dissatisfied with the outcome of a claim issue for an employee. The client knew we took the proper steps to resolve the issue, but still wasn't satisfied. When I asked what she expected the next step to be, she revealed that she wanted us to escalate the issue through another channel at the insurance carrier, which we proceeded to do.*
>
> *Even though the final outcome ultimately wasn't the result she wanted, the client was pleased because she felt we truly advocated on their behalf. Her expectations, as we learned, were more about the lengths to which she wanted us to push than they were about whether or not the claim was going to be paid; and I would never have known this if I didn't ask.*
> *-Bonnie A.*

How often has someone promised to get back to you with an answer but you failed to understand when? How often have you seen sloppiness around expectations with phrases like "It shouldn't take too long" or "I'll get back to you as soon as possible?" Phrases like these are vague and increase the chances for missed expectations. My definition of "before too long" or "as soon as possible" may be very different than yours. More importantly, I'm going to judge you based upon *my* expectation, not yours.

Learn to be clear and specific in setting expectations for your own performance and in asking for expectations

> *In customer service, we know that setting clear expectations for our callers is a key to ensuring satisfaction; and when we don't, we pay the price. One of our Employee Advocates (Service Representatives) was recently helping an employee who was waiting for reimbursement on a claim. The Employee Advocate asked him to complete a specific form and send it in.*
>
> *A week later, the employee went to HR upset because he hadn't received the reimbursement yet, even though these claims usually take several weeks for the insurance carrier to process. Our failure to set a clear expectation for him about how long it should take for reimbursement left him guessing and, ultimately, disappointed.*
> -Bonnie A.

of others. Phrases such as "I'll get back to you by noon tomorrow" or "I'll respond before the end of business today" are clear and reduce the risk of missed expectations. It's also important to be sure that the expectations we're setting are satisfactory to our customer. For example, we might say, "I'll get back to you by Wednesday afternoon. Will that be sufficient for you?" If that doesn't work for someone, at least we're engaging in a conversation about their expectations and creating some mutually acceptable agreement.

What happens if the customer's expectation is unreasonable? By talking about expectations upfront, we have the opportunity to alter their expectation or even come up with a counterproposal that would still meet their needs. Let's suppose they say they need an answer by this afternoon, but you know it will be impossible. You might ask if getting a portion of the answer by this afternoon would still accomplish their goals with the remaining part of the answer coming by tomorrow. The key is to create agreement about the expectation. Allowing the customer to have an unrealistic expectation that goes undisclosed is a prescription for certain failure.

There's simply no reason to guess about what people expect or require of us, or what we should expect of others. Just ask!

Recovery

Are you familiar with the customer service concept known as "recovery?" This concept suggests that when a service breakdown occurs, you have an extraordinary opportunity to create loyalty. Why is this? It all has to do with understanding the role of expectations.

Let me give you an example. You and your spouse go out to dinner and have a totally satisfactory meal, with reasonable service that meets your every expectation. You're entirely contented. Who do you tell? Probably no one. Now let's suppose you go to the same restaurant and your food is served cold or is otherwise lacking. You're disappointed, and you let the manager know this. The chef comes out and personally apologizes, brings out another dish, and promises that the meal will be without charge. The manager comes over to apologize and gives you a gift certificate to return and have your next meal "on the house," and asks you to notify him directly so that he can personally see to it that your next experience is an extraordinary one. Now who do you tell? Probably lots of people. Are you likely to come back? Absolutely. So what happened here and how does it relate to expectations?

Remember that we're going to judge the event not by what happens, but by how it compares to what we're expecting to happen. In the first example, you had fairly high expectations and they were met. There was relatively little opportunity to exceed the expectations because they were already fairly high. The result was satisfaction.

In the second example, once the poor meal was served, your expectations dropped. You no longer thought as highly of the restaurant. It must have been over-rated. With the "bar" now lowered, a greater opportunity was created to exceed the expectations. As your expectations were exceeded, you became more impressed and more likely to share stories of the experience with others, and more likely to return. It's fascinating to note that the restaurant is better off having disappointed you and then recovered, than if you had not ever been disappointed in the first place. (This is not to suggest that creating disappointments is a good idea—just that disappointments create golden opportunities for exceeding expectations). "Recovery" is all about capitalizing on lowered expectations.

Here's a recovery story I remember happening in our office. One of our consultants, I'll call him Mark, was due to meet with several employees of a client to offer investment advice. The meeting was set for 7:00 am. When the client called at 7:20 to find out why Mark hadn't arrived, we became concerned. It turned out that we had an internal miscommunication about the location, and Mark had been waiting at another one of the client's sites since 6:45. By the time the error was recognized, it was too late to meet with the employees. Expectations were missed. What did we do?

Within hours, we had gotten the home addresses of the affected employees and mailed a letter of apology to each, accepting full responsibility. We included a pair of movie tickets with each letter, asking the employee to enjoy a movie on us. We then rearranged a new time to meet. The client was thrilled, and our relationship was enhanced beyond where it would have been had the error not originally happened. We exceeded the expectations.

Getting to "Unbelievable"

One of the standards we often talked about at RSI was that of being "unbelievable." We didn't want customers to be "satisfied." Rather, we wanted them to be raving about us. To understand how to achieve this, I conducted a number of focus groups among our clients over a period of years. Here's what I discovered.

Responsiveness generates excellence. Proactivity generates "unbelievable." What most customers expect is responsiveness. Give the customer what they ask for when they ask for it. In other words, meet their expectations. If you do this, they'll regard you as excellent and maybe even outstanding. However, if you want to be regarded as "unbelievable," you have to surprise them. You have to exceed their expectations. The most common way to do this is by being proactive. Offer them additional value they had not expected.

Here's a challenge we often had at RSI with regard to customer expectations—and as you read this, think about the extent to which your business probably has the same issue. We knew, of course, that customers would judge us on how we did in meeting or exceeding their expectations, yet so often we had a multitude of people who each had a hand in the setting and delivering of those expectations.

We had sales executives who made promises or commitments on behalf of the organization. We had a client who would hear and interpret those commitments and internalize them in terms of expectations. Of course, the customer's own previous history of vendor relationships also played a role in the formation of their expectations. Then, we had consultants and service professionals who were primarily responsible for the delivery of the commitments made by the sales executive and interpreted by the customer. Do you notice a problem here? With so many people part of the expectation dynamic, the situation was fraught with opportunities for misunderstanding. What I also noticed was that virtually every case of missed expectations had at its core a misunderstanding or miscommunication about what was to happen.

So, how do you solve this? It's rather simple. You make sure that all key parties understand—in writing—the primary expectations of the customer. You create an "expectations document" that outlines—in writing—all the key commitments, promises, and expectations. You make sure that the sales executive, client, consultant, and service professional all discuss and sign off on their agreement. In this way, you can be sure that the expectations are clearly understood. Then you set up a quarterly meeting with the customer to get feedback on their perception of how you're delivering on the commitments. With these pieces in place, you dramatically reduce the chance that you fall short of expectations; after all, this is how you'll be judged. I'm almost embarrassed to admit how obvious a step this is and yet we operated for so many years without it.

I've been mostly talking about expectations from a customer and vendor perspective, but the issue is identical in all human interactions. Let's see how this applies to internal relationships.

Internal Expectations

A business organization is a collection of people working together toward a common objective. It's composed of a huge number of interdependent working relationships. Sales, service, operations, administration, and finance must all be able to interact with each other successfully. Every day, hundreds, if not thousands, of conversations take place where expectations are being created. A manager asks a team member for a report. A salesperson asks for a proposal to be created. An administrator asks a teammate to get an answer.

If we fail to ask for and set expectations, we leave it entirely to chance whether we meet the expectations of another. In every conversation we have, we need to learn to discuss expectations. Ask questions like these: "By when do you need this?" "How long will that take?" "When can you have that complete?" "I need this by Thursday. Will that be possible?" "If I have this to you on Tuesday, will that work for you?"

Notice that this Fundamental says "*set* and *ask for* expectations." Both are equally important, and both parties in an interaction have an equal responsibility in expectation setting. If you're the one providing the action or the service, you need to let the other person know what to expect. How will the task be done? When? Under what conditions? At what cost? If you're on the receiving end, you need to ask for the expectations, so that you can be certain you're both on the same page.

Why We Fail to Set Expectations

Here's something I've noticed often leads to a failure to ask for expectations: Too often we confuse asking for expectations with being demanding. I watched this take place often in my years at RSI. We would call an insurance carrier on behalf of a client, and the carrier contact would promise to look into the issue and get back to us. They would not tell us when, and we too often failed to ask. Why? Because for some, it feels pushy or demanding to say, "When will you get back to me with this answer?" It feels too confrontational. Of course, you know my point of view! This is not about confrontation or about being demanding. It's about *clarity*. If we're not both working from the same set of expectations because we're too afraid to discuss them upfront, we're simply inviting misunderstanding later.

> *As a salesperson, I've found that an invaluable step in each and every phase of the sales process is setting and asking for expectations. From the first phone call to the close of the sale, it's so important that my prospect and I are on the "same page."*
>
> *So much time is wasted on everyone's part if I don't take the time to clarify a prospect's expectations/intentions and determine mutually agreed upon expectations of what will happen next. Not doing so has resulted in, for example, several first appointments in which I prepared to go in and ask scores of questions while my prospect, however, believed that I was coming in to do a full presentation. Needless to say, neither of our expectations was met, and it was a disappointing interaction for everyone involved.*
>
> *I've learned to always determine the prospect's expectations, make sure I didn't miss or misunderstand anything, and make sure we're both in sync about the next steps. Taking the time to set and ask for expectations today reduces the opportunity for misunderstandings and unfulfilled expectations tomorrow.*
> *-Nancy N.*

Another reason we often fail to ask for expectations is that it feels too awkward. I see this especially in personal situations. I recently had a call from a friend who invited me to join him and two others on a golf trip because a spot had opened up when another person had to cancel at the last minute. I was available and wanted to go, but was unsure of the expectations around who was paying for what. He hadn't set any expectations, and I felt awkward about asking. Here's a tip I've found that can help in overcoming the awkwardness: simply acknowledge the feeling to the other person, and then dive right in! I called the friend, told him that I felt a little funny asking this, but I just needed clarification about who was paying for what part of the trip. He quickly apologized for not having made it clearer, answered the question, and we were both happy. Problem solved. No misunderstanding.

Think about misunderstandings you've had with others. I'll bet virtually every one of them was related to a disconnect around expectations. Let me repeat: We judge events not by what happens, but rather by how they compare to what we expected to happen. Nothing could be more important than agreeing upon a clear set of expectations in advance.

FUNDAMENTAL #15

Make voicemail a valuable tool.

Your voicemail greeting is an important opportunity to set expectations and create a mood. Update voicemail daily and create a warm, friendly style that makes callers want to speak with you.

I'd like you to envision a scenario. Really put yourself into the situation and notice the feelings and emotions you experience as I describe several different outcomes.

Here's the situation: You've got a big sales presentation tomorrow afternoon that, if successful, will make your year, but there's one critical piece of information you need from one of your suppliers. The person who has that information is Mary, your contact at the supplier. You dial her number and

1. Get her assistant, who says that Mary doesn't have voicemail but promises to leave a note on her desk.

2. Get the same voicemail greeting Mary always has, which announces that she must be on her phone or away from her desk.

3. Get Mary's voicemail greeting, which says that today is Monday (even though it's really Thursday) and asks you to leave a message.

4. Get an automated voice recording that announces that the mailbox is full and suggests you try again at another time, and then it disconnects.

5. Get a message recorded by Mary's assistant announcing that you've reached Mary's phone and asking you to leave a message.

Can you feel the frustration and the stress building? You have no way to be sure Mary is getting your message, and no idea when you'll be able to connect with her. And your sale is riding on it! Undoubtedly you've had experiences exactly like this.

Now here's the tougher question: Who have *you* left with exactly these feelings by how you manage your voicemail?

Let's try the scenario again. Suppose that when you dialed Mary's number you were greeted by Mary's always pleasant voice thanking you for calling. Her message let you know that it was, in fact, Thursday, and that she was out on appointments in the morning but would be returning by 1:00, and that she expected to be able to return your call before the end of the day. She also let you know her cell phone number in case your question needed an even faster response. Notice the obvious difference in your emotions!

This Fundamental is a great opportunity to apply and practice two previous Fundamentals (#11 and #14).

In Fundamental #11, I talked about the importance of "creating a feeling of warmth and friendliness in every client interaction." Think of your voicemail greeting as an interaction. When someone calls and listens to your message, it's as if they're speaking with you. What feeling are they getting from the conversation? Is it one that makes them feel cared for? One that makes them look forward to speaking with you? One that gives them a glimpse into your personality?

Since we update our greeting every day, it's easy to get stuck in a routine where our voice begins to sound too mechanical or impersonal, like the airline flight attendants reciting safety instructions. Be careful to sound "real" in your greeting. One suggestion that can help with this is to smile as you record your greeting and picture the person who's listening to you. This helps to give your voice a more personal quality.

I often told our people that if you didn't occasionally have someone leave you a message complimenting you on how nice your voicemail greeting was, then the greeting wasn't friendly enough.

In Fundamental #14, I explained why it's so critical to "set and ask for expectations." Your voicemail greeting is a powerful expectation-setting tool. If I leave you a message and your voicemail greeting never changes, I have no idea whether you're in or out, when you'll get the message, and most importantly, when I should expect your return

> *Prior to coming to RSI, I was one of those people who never updated my voicemail. I had three standard messages I used based on whether I was in or out of the office or on vacation. When I joined RSI, though, I had to learn to create a friendly greeting and update it daily.*
>
> *About 2 months after I started, something happened that showed me why this was so important. A vendor left me a voicemail message telling me just how "blown away" he was by my greeting. He mentioned how cheerful it was and how much he appreciated how specific I was about my schedule and when I'd be able to get back to him. He has now even started to do the same and it's made it way easier for us to work together. If I could only get all our vendors to do this, life would be so much simpler!*
> *-Christine A.*

call. Conversely, if I leave you a message and you update your voicemail greeting daily, letting callers know your schedule and your availability for return calls, then I know what to expect in terms of response time. Since I'm going to judge you not by what happens, but by how it compares to what I expected to happen, you can see how critical it is to use your daily voicemail greeting wisely.

Incidentally, if I left you a message today, and I know that you change your greeting daily, at least I'm certain that, in fact, you did *get* my message.

And let's be honest. None of us is so busy that we can't take 60 seconds each day to record and update our own voicemail greeting. Even if our schedule is packed, we can just record it in the evening before bed. There simply are no good excuses.

Here's a pet peeve of mine: Executives that have their assistant record their voicemail greeting for them. Maybe I'm the only one sensitive about this, but I think it sends the wrong message. It leaves the caller with the impression that the executive is far too busy, and thinks he's far too important, to handle a detail as small as a voicemail recording.

As the President of our company, that's certainly not the impression I wanted to create. I wanted callers to know that I cared, that I was accessible, and that their message was truly important to me. Remember what I said in Institutionalizing Values about the importance of leaders demonstrating the values. How can I expect my people to treat callers with warmth, friendliness, and responsiveness if I'm not a walking model for it?

One final thought on voicemail as a tool: When leaving a message for someone else, be as specific as possible. Simply leaving a message to call you back does little to advance the situation. The more specific you can be with your question or answer, the more that can be accomplished in a shorter amount of time.

Voicemail can either be an amazingly effective tool, or the bane of our existence. Make yours a valuable tool.

FUNDAMENTAL #16

Follow-up everything.

Internal and external clients rely on us and we rely on others. Record a follow-up date for every action and take responsibility for its completion.

Have you ever considered the fact that there are very few things in business we can do alone? No matter what our position, we rely on a variety of other people to play some role in the value chain.

If I'm an architect, I may have suppliers I rely on for product specifications, builders I rely on to bring my work to fruition, clients I rely on to make decisions, clerical staff I rely on to handle certain administrative responsibilities, and so on. If I'm a salesperson, I rely on my company to deliver the promises I make to prospects. I may rely on my shipping department to get the products out, my customer service department to answer the clients' questions, my support staff to put together proposals, and my suppliers to help fill orders. As a matter of fact, I'm not sure I can think of a single role—be it CFO, sales person, administrator, customer service, or tech support—where I'm not somehow connected to a host of other people in order to ultimately deliver value for the customer.

At RSI, this fact was even more pronounced because we were the ultimate "middlemen." We helped insurance companies to distribute their products to employers, and we helped employers to buy and use the right products from those insurance companies. Here's the issue: Because we were middlemen, there were very few problems we actually could solve on our own. Rather, most of the time we were dependent on our contacts to resolve issues on behalf of clients while we were relegated to being largely "message carriers." Our clients relied on us, though, to hold people accountable and see that the issues were brought to a successful conclusion. The key to this accountability was learning to follow-up on *everything*.

When we were told that a claim was being paid, we learned to find out when (see Fundamental #14 – Set and ask for expectations), and then follow-up to be sure it was actually completed. When we requested a quote, we made note of when it was due and then followed-up to be sure it came in on time. When we checked on a commission issue, we would follow-up to see that we got our answer and that the correction did, in fact, take place. When we requested a new health insurance ID card for an employee, we followed-up to make sure that it was ultimately received when promised.

To ensure that follow-ups take place and, more importantly, that all the promised tasks are completed on time, it helps to create some structure around our follow-ups (see Fundamental #28 – Have a bias for structure and rebar). This structure can be quite simple and unsophisticated, or far more automated. For example, a simple suspense system can be a great way to stay on top of outstanding items. You're told the claim will be paid by next Thursday, so you put a note in your suspense folder for next Thursday to call and confirm that it was, in fact, completed. If you have a suspense file for each day of the month, and put your follow-up items in the appropriate day, you need only to be in the habit of going through that suspense file each day to ensure that nothing is left outstanding.

Of course technology has enabled us to use a number of software solutions to have even more control over our follow-ups. For example, if you use a program like Outlook for managing your tasks, you can simply create a task called "follow up on xyz claim" with a due date of next Thursday. This way, the task automatically pops up on that day and you don't need to worry about remembering it. This makes keeping track of all the items you want to check on quite easy. Virtually every task management software program has a method for assigning tasks to particular days.

This issue was important enough that when we wrote a custom back-office software system, we programmed in a number of critical follow-up tools. As one example, whenever a customer service person (we called them "Employee Advocates" or EAs) took a phone call, they would type the details of the call into a screen in our system. If the issue was not completely resolved at that time, the EA would be forced to enter a follow-up date before exiting the screen. Each morning, when the EA logged into their system to start their day, a screen would come up showing all of their scheduled follow-ups for the day. These could even be organized by insurance carrier to make the calls easier and more efficient.

Whether you're more comfortable with a paper-based system or a technology-driven one, the key is developing the habit of logging follow-ups for everything. If you don't log it, how good your system is doesn't matter. Whenever a person promises to get something to you, get clear information about the due date and then put it into your follow-up system.

Sometimes I hear people complain that "we shouldn't have to check to be sure that promises are kept. It's such a waste of valuable time. We ought to be able to rely on others to honor their commitments." While I agree that it's a shame to have to spend our time this way, whether we should or shouldn't have to is truly irrelevant. The reality is that if we're to take responsibility (see Fundamental #23) for seeing that issues are resolved, we *must* be rigorous and unrelenting in our follow-up.

Remember that we all live in an interdependent world. While our clients count on us to see that results are achieved, we're dependent upon a variety of other people each doing their part so that we can ensure success. If anyone drops the ball at any point along the line, the promised result gets jeopardized. The rigor we bring to our follow-ups can mean the difference between success and failure. Develop the habit of following up on *all* your activities.

One of my jobs was to coordinate the filing of Form 5500 for our clients. This was a form that the federal government requires every company over a certain size to complete and file annually. In order to complete the form, we relied on the insurance carriers to supply part of the necessary information. They did this through what was known as a Schedule A. If the 5500s weren't filed in a timely way, our clients could be subject to significant penalties, so it was critical that we stay on top of the status of all forms at all times.

To help us do this, we created a grid where we logged all filings by the month they were due, and outlined each step taken. We used it daily to track where we stood and to follow up with every carrier if we had not received the Schedule A yet. Sometimes it required multiple follow-up calls, but it was the best way to ensure that everything was always done on time.
-Diane S.

FUNDAMENTAL #17

Be punctual.

Be on time for all appointments, phone calls, meetings, and promises. How you relate to time sends a message about how you relate to other commitments. Punctuality is a sign of respect for others.

When I reflect on this Fundamental, I think one of the reasons so many people struggle with punctuality is that they see it as a personal issue that really only affects themselves. If it didn't involve other people, what time you intend to do some things (get to the gym, go grocery shopping, send an e-mail, etc.) wouldn't matter all that much. However, when we recognize that most of our appointments involve shared commitments with other people, punctuality takes on a whole different perspective

When we have an appointment, whether that appointment is a group meeting, an individual meeting, or a phone call, we've entered into a commitment with someone else. Honoring our commitments (Fundamental #21) requires us to be on time. When we're on time, we show the world that we're serious about fulfilling our commitments. Conversely, sloppiness about being on time reflects a sloppiness or lackadaisical attitude about commitments in general.

Beyond the relationship between punctuality and commitment is the basic issue of courtesy. Being on time shows other people that we value and respect them. It shows that we consider their time to be important.

When we think about punctuality, we most often think about making sure that we show up on time for all scheduled appointments and meetings. There's no question these are critical, but there are other facets of how we manage our time in relation to others that are equally important. Let's take a look at just a few of those aspects.

Leading Meetings

How frustrating is it to show up on time for a meeting only to have it start 20 minutes late? You've shown respect for the others attending the meeting as well as the leader, but now they're wasting your time. Be conscious as a meeting leader to start all meetings at their scheduled time. If some people don't show up on time, start the meeting anyway and later ask for their commitment to be prompt for all future meetings. Otherwise you're creating a culture where lateness is acceptable behavior.

Just as frustrating as having meetings start late is having meetings end late. There's nothing like having a meeting scheduled for 9:00-10:00 and then have it run till 10:45. In my experience, the primary reason for this, outside of starting late, is that conversations are allowed to continue when they're either not relevant for this particular meeting or are past the point of being productive. How many times have you sat through meetings where the same point was repeated at length multiple times?

If you're the leader of the meeting, it's your responsibility to manage the discussion so that it's relevant and productive. And if you're a participant, you also have a responsibility to see that your contributions are appropriate.

One of the simplest and most effective tools for running a meeting on time is to have a clear agenda with specific amounts of time allotted to each topic. It's amazing the impact that having times attached to the agenda can have. I used to be the President of the Board for a large non-profit social service agency. Prior to my taking over, Board meetings had a history of going on forever as discussion on each topic would become repetitive and unproductive. When I instituted the practice of having time allocations next to each agenda item, it was fascinating to watch people become much more sensitive to how long discussions went on.

Obviously, there are times when important issues are being discussed and additional time is necessary and appropriate. In these situations, as the leader, you should check in with the participants to see if everyone can spend the additional time, and if not, what other arrangements can be made. This, once again, demonstrates respect for everyone's time.

Conducting Sales Calls

When we make sales calls, our prospect has agreed to set aside a certain amount of time to meet with us. Just as it's important to show up at the scheduled time, it's also important to manage the call in the allotted time. Our sales reps would often check in with the prospect about 2/3 of the way through the meeting to make sure that they were comfortable with the pace and the time remaining. Here again, if both parties agree to extend the time, going longer is fine. Being conscious of the time is a way of showing respect for the other person. Of course, this same principle applies to other one-on-one appointments beyond sales calls.

Completing Tasks

When we promise to complete a task for someone by a certain date or at a certain time, it's really the same as an appointment. We've made a commitment and set an expectation. It's imperative that we regard this commitment with the same seriousness that we regard a physical appointment. If, for some reason, we anticipate trouble in meeting the deadline, courtesy demands that we let the other person know at the earliest possible moment so that alternative plans can be made, as applicable.

This notion of letting others know if a commitment can't be met, of course, obviously holds true for physical appointments as well. We need to organize ourselves around being on time by reasonably allowing for possible contingencies. However, if something unforeseen occurs that will make us late, naturally we have a responsibility to let those affected know as soon as possible.

Without question, the absolute worst offenders in this regard are doctors' offices. For some reason, most of us have accepted that it's OK to be kept waiting 30 or 60 minutes past our appointment time just because that's what happens in doctors' offices. There's no reason at all that the office couldn't and shouldn't call patients to let them know they're running behind and thereby allow everyone to adjust their schedules accordingly. It's a demonstration of courtesy and respect.

The Importance of "Always"

I sometimes hear people dismiss occasional tardiness by saying that they're "usually" or "often" punctual. The problem with punctuality being less than "always" is that I don't know in advance whether this is one of those situations where you *will* be on time or one where you *won't* be. It goes back to expectations (Fundamental #14). Unless you're always on time, I simply don't know what to expect.

Work to make punctuality an unwavering part of how you operate.

SECTION 3

The Collaborative Way – These practices enable us to work powerfully together as a team.

In 1996, I was introduced to a collection of practices that was to have a significant impact on how I viewed communication, both personally and in our business. These practices, known as The Collaborative Way, were developed by Lloyd Fickett, a management consultant who had worked with several of my peers. Beginning in February of that year, I, along with my brother Larry and one of our managers, spent a full day each month for two years learning the nuances of these practices from Lloyd, developing our own skills as we prepared to roll them out to our company.

Fundamentals #18 through #22 are five of those practices. While the discussions that follow reflect my own learning and experiences, the specific language of these practices was authored by Lloyd. With his invaluable guidance, we've taught these tools to every one of our staff since 1998, principally in the format of a two-day off-site intensive experience. Not only has the Collaborative Way had a powerful and lasting impact on our company, but Larry has also taught this program to hundreds of people outside of RSI as well.

(Note: For more information about Lloyd Fickett, Lloyd Fickett & Associates, Inc., and The Collaborative Way, see http://thecollaborativeway.com)

FUNDAMENTAL #18

Listen generously.

Learn to listen for the contribution in each other's speaking versus listening from our assessment, opinions, and judgments.

This is the first of five Fundamentals that encompass the core practices of The Collaborative Way. It's truly amazing to witness the impact that the *way* in which we listen has on *what* we actually hear; and *what* we actually hear, in turn, has a significant influence on how we respond to situations. As a matter of fact, as we look more deeply into this Fundamental, you may be surprised to see that our listening has more opportunity to impact outcomes than even our speaking.

Another Look at Filters

Before we begin our exploration, however, it'll be useful for us to take another look at the discussion we had about "filters" in Fundamental #9. There I described a filter as a conceptual device that alters the way in which we receive sensory data, much like a pair of eyeglasses. Well, the impact of our filters is even greater when it comes to our listening. We all have ways of listening that influence and color what we hear. We sometimes call this "automatic listening" because it happens by habit, often without us being consciously aware that we're doing it. Let me give you a few examples to show you what I mean.

- You've always found Susan to be a "whiner." She constantly seems to have a complaint about something, and it's usually unfounded or petty. As she knocks on your door to tell you about her latest issue, you listen through the filter of "I already know that what she has to say has little merit."

- Whenever Tom returns from a sales call, he reports that the deal is likely to close soon, but it rarely does. Tom has asked if you have a minute for him to tell you about the call he was on this morning. As you listen, you hear him through the filter of "Tom always exaggerates the success of his calls."

- You believe that your sister has always had a chip on her shoulder about people who've graduated from college, because she never did. As she tells you about how the job she wanted went to a college graduate instead of her, you listen through the filter of "My sister always blames her lack of success on everyone but herself."

- You believe that management is only interested in advancing their careers through short-term successes, even if it's to the long-term detriment of the organization. As your manager rolls out the latest change initiative, you listen through the filter of "I know this is a bad idea and he's only doing this so he can look good."

Notice how automatic these filters are. Because we have experience with certain people, and we think we know "how they are," it becomes terribly difficult for us to clear our minds and truly listen generously to what they have to say. Often, our filters aren't necessarily about other specific people, but are about our own world view. Consider these examples:

- You believe that all people can achieve success if they're willing to work hard enough. When someone complains about not having opportunity, you listen to them through the filter of "They're just lazy and unwilling to accept responsibility for their situation."

- You believe that everyone should volunteer their time to serve their community. When your neighbor declines to work on the PTA fundraiser because she's busy with work and kids, you listen to her through the filter of "There are no good excuses. We all must do our part."

I want to be clear that we *all* have filters. None of us is totally able to listen with a completely blank slate; filters are part of being human. We naturally use our past experiences and our beliefs to influence how we hear and process information. Having a filter is not the problem. Failing to recognize it is.

When we don't notice or own our filters as being just that, we begin to think that what we're hearing is "reality." In other words, we think of it as the only truth. However, as we become more sensitive or aware of our automatic listening, we open up space for listening more generously and more curiously, and we become open to many more possibilities. We're able to see a larger, more nuanced picture of people and events. Ultimately, it's about giving ourselves more flexibility and choice in how we respond.

Additional Listening Challenges

If you've ever really worked at it, you know that good listening is an active process, not a passive one. It requires us to be truly engaged. I've found that one of the most difficult challenges to being a good listener is learning to quiet our minds. Too often, the conversation in our own heads gets in the way of our capacity to really hear the richness in what the other person is trying to communicate. Here are a few habits that most of us tend to struggle with that limit the quality of our listening:

- **Listening from judgment.** This is one of the hardest ones for me. I so often find myself listening to determine how much I agree or disagree with the speaker. I do this especially when I'm in a seminar, but it's also a habit in my everyday listening. The voice in my head is so busy judging what I'm hearing, that it interferes with my ability to absorb the full meaning of what's being said.

- **Listening just to give the other person a chance to speak.** Often, we confuse listening with just letting the other person have their chance to say something. It's more like "not speaking" than it is listening. We simply stop using our voice for a few minutes and give the other person an opportunity to use theirs, but are we really listening? Or are we just taking turns speaking?

- **Listening with our minds made up.** Have you ever allowed another person to "have their say" but you're already locked in on your point of view? When our mind is already made up, we become rigid and inflexible and we miss out on the potential contributions that may be available in what the other person has to offer. Moreover, when the other person notices this, they usually shut down, recognizing that they're simply wasting their breath.

- **Listening when we think we already know what the other person is going to say.** This is another one the speaker can usually detect. Think about times when people have listened to you this way. How does it make you feel? I find it makes me feel trapped, as if the other person is only hearing their own predetermined message and not getting what I'm really trying to say. Sometimes this also shows up in the habit of finishing other people's sentences for them, rather than allowing them the chance to completely articulate what they intend.

So far, we've been looking at what listening generously is *not,* and what gets in the way of our ability to listen generously, but we haven't yet examined what it *is.* Let's turn to that now, and then we'll consider a few tips for practicing our skills, before we conclude by looking at how listening generously can influence action.

What is Generous Listening?

The best way I can describe generous listening is to say that it's listening for the contribution in another's speaking. It's listening fully, looking for the most positive way to hear the other person. Lloyd Fickett, the author of The Collaborative Way, identifies the following attributes of what it looks like when we're listening generously:

- **Giving our full attention to the speaker.** How often do we listen while doing something else at the same time —reading, looking at our computer, typing an e-mail, watching TV? Sometimes we may not be *doing* something else, but we're *thinking* something else—thinking about what we're going to say when this person is done, or thinking about something entirely different like what else we have to do today. Only when the speaker has our full and complete attention can we actively engage our listening in the most generous way.

- **Being curious and willing to be influenced**. I find this to be one of the truest tests of generous listening. Are we truly willing to be influenced? Can we set aside all of our beliefs and opinions and become curious enough to really understand completely what the other person is saying? Can we literally be open to the possibility that we might change our point of view based on what we hear, or are we listening merely to be polite and allow the other person to "have their say?" When we can allow this possibility, we open ourselves to amazing insights and new options and alternatives.

- **Setting aside our prejudices, preconceived conclusions, and judgments**. This goes back to our discussion of filters. To listen generously, we first need to recognize and own our preconceived notions. Once we realize our inclination to have our "automatic listening" turned on, we can work to turn it off. Turning off or setting aside our preconceptions opens the pathway for us to genuinely hear the value in what's being said by another.

- **Not waiting for an opening to argue our point or think of a rebuttal**. I know I struggle with this one frequently, and it's an easy trap to fall into. Instead of truly hearing what the other person is saying and digesting it fully, a portion of our mind is two steps ahead, thinking about our response or the counterpoint to what's being said. We sometimes think of conversations like a chess game, where our goal is to anticipate the other person's moves and plan our counterattack. Listening generously, though, requires us to quiet our minds and pay full and complete attention to understanding what the speaker is saying.

It's important to point out that listening generously is more than just listening objectively. Much like working from the assumption that people are good, fair, and honest (Fundamental #9), listening generously implies that we're assuming positive intent. We're looking for the most positive way to hear another person. We're looking for the contribution to our own thinking or understanding that the speaker can offer.

It's also important to be clear that generous listening has nothing at all to do with agreeing. Rather, it's about understanding. Our goal in our listening is to come to as complete an understanding as possible of what the speaker is trying to communicate. To that end, let's consider a few tips that can help us to listen more generously.

Tips for Listening More Generously

- **Eliminate distractions**. It's awfully hard to listen generously when we're distracted by outside influences. Put away the cell phone, put down the book or newspaper, stop looking at the computer, and focus your complete attention on the speaker.

- **Replicate**. Listen for the essence of what the speaker is saying and give it back to them in your own words. "So if I'm understanding you correctly, what you're saying is…" Or, "It sounds like what you're telling me is…" These kinds of statements not only give you the opportunity to check to see if you're getting it, but they also give the speaker the chance to make any slight corrections. "That's almost correct, but I'm also saying that…" In addition to this clarifying process, you're demonstrating to the speaker that you're listening carefully and wanting to understand.

- **Quiet the voices in your head**. Notice how many conversations are taking place in your mind as you listen. How many things are you thinking about besides what's being said? Practice taming those voices and focus solely on listening to the person you're with.

Listening generously is hard work, and it takes practice; but the impact we can have with our listening is significant—both on ourselves as well as on others.

The Impact of Listening

As I mentioned earlier, when we minimize our automatic listening, we're able to hear things that would otherwise not get through our filter. This gives us a much broader view of situations and people, and this broader view gives us greater choices for how we approach nearly everything. When my point of view is narrow and rigid, I'm limited in my options. When my point of view becomes expanded and flexible, I increase the range of possibilities many times over. Our listening also influences the actions of other people.

The more fully we listen, the more we cause others to open up, to contribute, and to blossom. Think about how you feel when it seems as though your boss is not listening when you speak. You're likely to feel less valued, less important. And our typical response to these feelings is to shut down. Why bother telling the boss about your idea if she doesn't listen anyway? In fact, why bother even thinking creatively, since she already knows the answer to everything and doesn't even pay attention to anyone else?

Now think of the opposite. How do you feel when your boss gives you his undivided attention, asking questions to clarify, really trying to understand just what you have in mind? Naturally, you're likely to feel validated, excited, enthusiastic, appreciated. And, of course, our response to these feelings is to think of more great ideas, to be creative, to try new approaches to solving a problem.

Notice how totally different our actions are likely to be based solely on whether we felt listened to or not listened to. Being listened to does have a powerful impact on us.

Let's take this one step further. Think of the difference in collaboration and, ultimately, success when an organization is able to create an environment that encourages and supports generous listening. How much more creative are people likely to be? How much more engaged are they likely to be? How much more receptive to new approaches are they likely to be? How many more good ideas are likely to surface? The difference is truly enormous.

Yes, generous listening is *that* powerful. Open yourself up to this practice and watch what happens around you.

FUNDAMENTAL #19

Speak straight.

Speak honestly in a way that forwards what we are up to. Make clear and direct requests. Be willing to surface ideas or take positions that may result in conflict when it's necessary to reach our objectives.

This is the second of the Collaborative Way practices, and is the one that I observe people struggle with the most. So what is "speaking straight" and why is it so difficult?

Speaking straight is being direct, clear, and honest in our communication. However, it's important to recognize that speaking straight is not simply "dumping our bucket" on others or being brutally honest without regard to the way in which we deliver our message. Rather, speaking straight includes the concept of "forwarding" what we're up to. It's being direct, but in a way that enables the other person to truly hear us and that improves the likelihood of positive movement toward our team objectives. The whole point of speaking straight is to forward the action. It therefore requires an extraordinary amount of thoughtfulness as well as a deep commitment to being "for each other."

Like so many of the Fundamentals, this can sound so simple, but it actually goes much deeper than it may at first seem. Let's peel back the onion a bit to examine some of its components more closely, and I think you'll see just what I mean.

Honest

Speaking straight is always honest. It's authentically communicating what you're thinking or feeling, rather than lapsing into political correctness or social politeness. It's speaking your mind candidly rather than withholding your contribution in favor of silence. (Before I go on here, let me remind you that speaking straight comes with a responsibility to be "forwarding." It's not just telling others what you think. More on that just ahead...)

Imagine you're in a strategic planning meeting with the executive team. Your boss is extolling the virtues of the new company direction and why he thinks it's the right course of action. He's clearly excited about his plan, and asks if anyone has a problem with his analysis. Truth be told, you have significant reservations and think this is a real mistake, but you're concerned about disagreeing with the boss. What do you do?

Faced with this situation, most people will either remain silent or will say they're in agreement, even though it's not the truth. There are a variety of reasons for this, which we'll explore. But for now, think about the impact that *not* speaking straight can have. In this example, it could allow a company to make a potentially serious and costly strategic mistake for lack of a robust, honest, intellectual exchange. Think about all of the honest conversations that *aren't* taking place in your work environment and consider the staggering potential cost!

By the way, consider as well the wasted time and energy spent on conversations where people are less than honest with each other. I ask you if you can work late on Thursday evening. You say that it's "no problem" but you make a face as you say it and your body language says otherwise. You're hoping I'll read your signs and understand that it's really not OK, and you're disappointed when I don't. You walk away disgruntled, telling others that I don't listen to you. If we're speaking straight, you give me a clear and honest answer to my question and we discuss it openly and candidly. Our chances of a successful resolution are dramatically increased; and it's faster!

Forwarding

Speaking straight is always forwarding. This is a critical component to understand, and it's what distinguishes speaking straight from simply dumping.

When I use the word "forwarding," I'm referring to creating positive movement toward an objective. For example, referring back to the strategic planning meeting, it would not be forwarding to simply state that you think the boss's idea is stupid (never mind the ramifications!). However, identifying the specific areas in which you have concern, and even suggesting some alternative approaches, would be very forwarding. You've contributed to the conversation in a productive way that promotes further dialogue and positive action.

How about this one: Imagine that you overhear your co-worker on the phone having a conversation with her mother. As you listen, you're annoyed and disturbed by how rudely she appears to be speaking. When she gets off the phone, you honestly let her know how obnoxious you think she was. Is this speaking straight?

Unless there's some greater purpose beyond simply expressing your disgust, this is *not* an example of straight speaking. It's critical to understand that we don't *always* have to say whatever is on our mind. Remember that the purpose of speaking straight is to forward what we're up to. Many times, what's on our mind is not at all forwarding. In these cases, silence is far more useful. Dishonesty, however, is never an appropriate choice.

Said in a Way That Can Be Heard

Speaking straight is always done in a way that can more easily "be heard." Have you ever noticed that the *way* in which a message is delivered to you has a significant impact on how or even *whether* you receive it? I find that when it sounds to me like people are whining or complaining, it's very difficult for me to hear what they have to tell me. However, when they approach things from a "win/win" perspective, it's much easier for me to hear them and, in turn, I become much more receptive to whatever they have to say.

Picture this scenario: You're the sales manager and you've just accompanied one of your reps on a sales call. You were pretty disappointed in his performance. In fact, some of what you witnessed actually made you cringe. When you get back into the car, you let him have it. You point out all the things he did wrong, and berate him for being so stupid. You let him know how disappointed you are that he's still making these kinds of mistakes at this point in his career. Did you speak straight?

You were honest; I'll give you that! But remember, speaking straight is not about simply telling people your honest opinion. What you're "up to" in this situation is helping your sales rep to improve his performance. In fact, if you're really for his success, you have a responsibility to speak honestly with him about your observations; but speaking straight also requires that you do it in a way that he can hear. How do you think he might react if instead of berating him, you showed him specifically how you'd like him to handle the same issues in the next call, and then had him practice the new approach with you? You're still being honest, and you're helping to forward the action by speaking to him in a way that he can more easily hear you.

Clear

Speaking straight is always clear. Think of a master chef and the tools of his trade. He has a specific type of knife for every purpose, and they're always sharp. For most of us, we spend more of our time communicating than anything else—speaking, listening, writing, and reading. Words are our tools, and we need to use them with the same precision with which the master chef uses his knives. It's remarkable how much misunderstanding comes as a direct result of sloppiness around our language. Let me give you an example.

One of the most common misunderstandings I see is in relation to requests. A good request involves an asker, a responder, a set of criteria for fulfilling the request, an agreed upon time period, and a committed response. Consider these two scenarios:

> Scenario 1: I ask you if you can get me the monthly sales report. You say you'll see what you can do.

> Scenario 2: I ask you to get me the monthly sales report by the end of the day on Tuesday. You say that you cannot do that because you've got a big presentation to prepare for on Monday; and you ask if it would be OK to get it to me by noon on Wednesday. I accept your counter-offer.

Notice the lack of precision in the first scenario. I didn't actually ask you to get me the report. I asked you "if" you can get it to me. I didn't specify when and you made no commitment as to what you will do. While this may sound picky, notice what can happen. I'm inaccurately relating to the request as a commitment and am disappointed when it's not done by whatever date was in my mind. I may even have counted on getting it in time to compile a larger report that I need to submit to our Board by the end of the week. You're thinking you'll just try to squeeze it in whenever you have a chance. Our lack of precision allows us to have a differing set of expectations, with potentially serious consequences.

In the second scenario, I've made a very clear request and I've specified the time by which I'm expecting completion. You've clearly declined my request and suggested a counterproposal. I've accepted that proposal. We both know exactly what is to be delivered and by when.

While the example I've given you is about a simple report, you can readily see how these same misunderstandings can occur around a variety of issues, large and small. Expanded over the course of an entire company and all the conversations taking place each day and each year, the cost of this lack of precision becomes quite meaningful.

When we speak straight, we're clear and accurate, and say precisely what we mean. Our purpose is to forward what we're up to; and to that end, we're always honest. We're thoughtful about the way we deliver our message, always being careful to do so in a way that's more likely to be able to be heard by the listener.

What Gets in the Way?

I noted earlier that I've found this to be one of the more difficult of the Collaborative Way practices for most people to do, myself included. Why is this so hard? Think about times in which you've not been straight with others and ask yourself "why?" Let's look at the most common challenges people have. See if you recognize any of these reasons.

1. Fear of confrontation or conflict. Most people find situations that may include personal conflict to be uncomfortable, so they avoid them. If I tell you that I need you to do a better job on the presentation materials, I'm afraid you'll argue with me about not having the resources and we'll just have a big fight about it. Instead, I'll just avoid the conversation and try to find some "workaround."

2. Fear of hurting someone's feelings. Often we're hesitant to be honest with someone because we're afraid that it might hurt their feelings or we're afraid of risking our relationship. Paradoxically, we actually honor the relationship greater by being straight than we do by avoiding difficult conversations. It's also interesting to note that most of us, if asked, would say that we'd prefer people tell us the truth, even when it's uncomfortable. And yet we don't do this with others.

3. Fear of how we'll be perceived. Many times we withhold our contribution for fear of how we may be perceived by others. We may not want to be seen as the "roadblock" to a course of action that has momentum, even if we have a significant concern. Or, we may fear that others will perceive us as having ulterior motives.

4. Perceived lack of authority. Sometimes we don't speak up because we don't believe we have the authority to do so. This is most common in superior-subordinate situations. If you're talking to your boss, you may feel that it's inappropriate to voice a dissenting opinion. Once again, of course, good bosses actually depend on honest feedback from the "front lines" in order to make better decisions. If this feedback is withheld, it can have serious consequences for the organization.

5. Fear of repeating a bad previous experience. There's nothing like a bad experience for getting us to avoid taking action. If the last time you thought you spoke honestly to your co-worker she went home crying or she chewed your head off, you're likely to be hesitant to try again.

> *Several years ago, I found myself agonizing over a conversation I knew I needed to have. It was about my compensation, and it was with the President of our company. It always feels awkward to me to talk about compensation, but I felt that I was being paid significantly less than others in our company who played a similar role and had similar experience. It was eating at me, and I knew I needed to deal with it.*
>
> *Thankfully, ours is an environment where "speaking straight" is both encouraged and expected. When I met with the President, I let him know that I felt uncomfortable bringing it up, but he encouraged me to be honest and listened intently. In the end, we had a great conversation, my compensation was adjusted to a place that we both felt was fair, and I felt so glad that I addressed the issue rather than letting it fester.*
> *-Christine G.*

6. Lack of a safe environment. One of the most important things you can do as a leader to promote straight speaking is to create a "safe" environment for doing so. This means that people are encouraged to be honest, are supported when they do so, and are never denigrated for what they have to say. When people don't feel it's safe to speak up, they'll either remain silent or they'll only tell you want they think you want to hear. Both are damaging.

It Takes Courage

In my experience, it often takes a great deal of courage to speak straight. Undoubtedly, there are conversations we all need to have that we've been avoiding. They may be personal ones or they may be work-related, but we all have them. They're the ones that give us that queasy feeling in our stomachs when we think about them. In fact, that's usually a pretty good sign that it's a conversation we need to have.

When approaching a difficult conversation, a helpful technique is to acknowledge to the other person your discomfort or awkwardness. "This is really difficult for me to talk about, but…" Or, "I don't want this to come across the wrong way, but…" By acknowledging this upfront, you can free yourself to have the conversation with less fear about the words not coming out precisely how you wanted. The listener is more apt to be able to "listen generously" and to work with you to be sure that you understand each other clearly.

Another technique that can be helpful is to create a hypothetical "rubber room." Just like a room with rubber walls reduces the risk of injury, our hypothetical rubber room is a safe place to have a difficult conversation. It's where you and a partner go where you both agree that nothing that's said will harm your relationship. With the safety of your relationship guaranteed, you're both more free to express yourselves with greater honesty.

When you think about all the individual conversations that take place each day, each week, and each year in your organization, and you consider the difference it can make when these conversations take place with honesty, clarity, and precision in a way that forwards the action, you get some sense of just how powerful this Fundamental can be. When we're in the habit of being straight with each other, team effectiveness skyrockets.

> *A number of years ago, when I went on maternity leave to have my daughter, I had an experience that really showed me the value of speaking straight and of "cleaning up" my messes. As an executive assistant, I was proud of my ability to keep my boss well-prepared and organized. Though I was going to be on leave, I expected to stay in touch, as I wanted to be sure that everything still went smoothly for him, and that it would be an easy transition when I returned.*
>
> *During my leave, however, my boss had very little communication with me. I felt excluded and unwanted and became resentful. I kept this resentment with me when I returned, and our relationship suffered. Finally, I realized I needed to speak straight and get to the bottom of it.*
>
> *What I discovered is that my boss thought he was doing me a favor by allowing me the time and space to attend to my family; meanwhile, I thought he didn't value me because of the way he was keeping his distance! Once we cleaned up our differences, our relationship was able to flourish once again. That experience taught me not to wait so long to speak straight when I know there's an issue that needs to be addressed.*
> *-Tina L.*

FUNDAMENTAL #20

Be for each other.

Support each other's success. Operate from the point of view that we're all in this together and that any one of us cannot win at the expense of someone else or the enterprise. Look for each other's greatness and provide rigorous support when needed.

One of my favorite times at RSI was when a new sale would be announced. You could always tell when this was happening by the hootin' and hollerin' coming out of the sales area and by the sound of the "moose." The moose, you see, was a stuffed animal head mounted on a plaque that would belt out a version of the song "I Feel Good" whenever its button was pushed. Often, the team members would join in the song and dance around their work stations. To see the genuine shared sense of joy that the sales team felt when any one of them succeeded was always a great demonstration of this Fundamental.

As perhaps you've found in your own experience, many organizations are saddled with an "every man for himself" culture. Often fueled by ego, each person is out to grab as much success (and credit) for himself as possible, regardless of its impact on others or on the organization as a whole. Sometimes, our reward systems even serve to support this type of attitude by incenting

> *As the IT specialist, one of my jobs is to respond to requests to resolve computer issues. One day, I got a message from an employee asking me to look at her computer. When I checked it out, I discovered that it really wasn't a hardware issue, so I couldn't help her. I started to leave her a message to this effect when I literally stopped mid-sentence. I realized that I wasn't really "being for her."*
>
> *It occurred to me that the goal is to help her solve her problem, not to tell her why it's not my job. After all, isn't that the whole point? So, I left her a new message explaining the situation and suggesting a variety of ways that I might be able to help her, even though they were beyond my normal scope of responsibility. Ultimately, together we were able to figure out a way to get her issue resolved, and she was so thankful for my support.*
> *-Jason Y.*

personal success without regard to team goals. In fact, it's the very reason I've long been a proponent of having a significant portion of bonus compensation be based on team or company goals, rather than purely individual ones.

I mentioned in Fundamental #9 that we practiced Open Book Management at RSI, sharing financial information and profits with our staff. As a part of this program, I designed the bonus payment to be a function of our company's net new sales results (sales minus losses) and overall profit. Based on our results, a pile of money would be allocated for distribution. We called this POCLO, for Pile of Cash Left Over. Most importantly, POCLO was distributed equally among all employees, regardless of position. The reason this was so important was that it helped everyone to see that we win and lose as a team. The impact of this approach was apparent every day.

Following are just a few examples of being for each other to help you get a clearer picture.

- Our busiest time of the year was usually around our clients' annual open enrollment. This was when employees made choices about their employee benefit plans, selecting the coverage they would have for the year. To prepare for this, we often put together comprehensive enrollment packets explaining the benefit plans and their costs. On our end, this meant hours of copying, collating, stapling, and stuffing papers in envelopes.

  The primary person responsible for this work was our consulting support specialist (CSS). It was not unusual to see a CSS send an e-mail to all staff asking for anyone available to help prepare packages to meet in our workroom. For the next several hours, we'd have 10 or 12 people from all positions—sales, service, management, consulting—standing around a large counter collating and stuffing packages. No one said, "It's not my problem." Rather, they all pitched in to support one another, and in so doing, support the team.

- There's nothing like going away on vacation only to return to a pile of work that's accumulated in your absence. The anticipation can sometimes be enough to ruin the last few days of vacation. At RSI, in most of our support positions, staff would step up to cover for each other when someone went on vacation. This meant that you were able to go away and truly enjoy your vacation, knowing that you'd find a relatively clean desk upon your return.

- I highlighted the sales team earlier in this chapter. No part of a company is typically as much of an "individual sport" as is sales. Each person has a very specific numeric goal to achieve, and the bulk of their compensation is based on its attainment. Sales people tend to be the most competitive and driven people in most organizations. And it's for all these reasons that I was always so proud to see the "team first" attitude portrayed by our team.

I would often see a sales rep return from a call and ask for advice from his teammates. It was not unusual to see them all huddled around a desk, strategizing about how one rep could handle a challenging prospect situation, sharing what's worked for them in the past. Sometimes they would even go on calls together. Here's the key thing: each one of them was competitive and desperately wanted to be the number one rep—but never at the expense of a teammate. They each genuinely pulled for each other and enthusiastically rooted for each other's success.

- In many companies, service staff view new sales as nothing more than a burden. It means additional work and little to no personal benefit. At RSI, though, new sales meant a greater chance to earn POCLO and a larger bonus for everyone. This caused everyone, in every position, to be acutely aware of our sales (and retention) efforts, and to offer to help in any way that they could. At times, one of our Employee Advocates would even accompany a sales rep on a prospect call if it might help to make a sale. Sometimes, an EA would work to solve a claim problem for a prospect just to increase the chances of getting the sale.

Demonstrating Support

While I've so far been describing "being for each other" mostly in terms of chipping in to help each other, there's another whole aspect of this Fundamental that's important to understand. Sometimes being for each other requires us to do difficult things. As I described in Fundamental #19, speaking straight with someone can, at times, be awkward and uncomfortable; yet if we're really for them, being straight with them is a better demonstration of support than avoidance is.

Being for someone is *not* about being nice or about being their friend. It's about doing everything you can to support their success. Suppose you have an employee whose performance is lacking. If you're truly for their success, you have a responsibility to address the issue head-on and help them to improve. Avoiding the situation or downplaying the performance gap is *not* being supportive.

At times, the most supportive thing you can do for a struggling employee is to help them separate from the company. Whenever we'd discuss an employee who was failing, I'd remind our managers that, being for our employees, we needed to do everything we reasonably could to ensure their success, rather than simply waiting for them to fail. However, at the earliest point at which we feel success is not possible, it becomes our responsibility to support the person by helping them to transition to life beyond RSI.

How about when someone isn't "struggling," but you know they could do better? Being for each other means that we demand of each other nothing short of our best. If I'm really for your success, I won't allow you to skate by, doing an adequate job when you're capable of doing so much more. Instead, I'll push you to perform at your highest level.

I sometimes think of being for each other as the "glue" that holds a team together; for it's impossible for a team to be highly functioning without teammates who rigorously support one another. And it's impossible for an organization to succeed without extraordinary teamwork.

FUNDAMENTAL #21

Honor commitments.

Do what you say you're going to do when you say you're going to do it. If a commitment cannot be fulfilled, notify others early and agree upon a new commitment to be honored.

If we're to work successfully with other people, I don't think there's a more important Fundamental than this one. You need to be able to rely upon me to do what I say I'll do, and I need to be able to rely upon you as well. Every time. Without fail. Think about the kind of organizational speed and interpersonal power that comes from the ability to count on each other without a second thought.

In Fundamental #1, I referred to Stephen M.R. Covey's insightful book, The Speed of Trust. Covey identifies 13 behaviors that are instrumental in creating trust, one of which is "keep commitments." Calling it "the 'Big Kahuna' of all behaviors," he goes on to observe this about keeping commitments:

> It's the quickest way to build trust in any relationship—be it with an employee, a boss, a team member, a customer, a supplier, a spouse, a child, or the public in general. Its opposite—to break commitments or violate promises—is, without question, the quickest way to destroy trust.

Let's take a closer look at the role that honoring commitments plays in building trust, and then we'll examine what it means to honor a commitment, as well as the primary reason many people frequently fall short of doing so.

Building Trust

Think about someone you trust more than anyone else you know. What words would you use to describe the nature of your relationship? People will typically identify things like these:

- I know I can rely on him
- I believe her
- She always keeps her promises
- He does what he says he'll do
- She's always there for me
- I know he'll always do the right thing

Notice how many of these comments relate to honoring commitments. Says Covey, "In almost any discussion of trust, keeping commitments comes up as the number one influencing factor."

At RSI, it was important for our account executives and consultants to build relationships with key contacts at our clients. Contrary to what some might suggest, building quality business relationships does not start with personal connections or finding points of common interest. Those are nothing more than social skills that create social relationships. Solid business relationships are built upon a foundation of trust, and trust is built upon the practice of honoring commitments.

In fact, when trying to establish a new relationship, the advice I often gave our consultants was to find some commitments you can make and keep—just to begin making deposits into the "trust bank account." Even small commitments help. Rather than saying, "I'll find out that answer," it's better to say, "I'll find out that answer and call you with it this afternoon before 3:00." Or, instead of saying, "I'll check on your new benefit booklets," I'd rather say, "I'll call you tomorrow morning to give you the status of the booklets, and I'll e-mail you with an update each Friday morning until I know they're in your hands." Obviously, having made the commitment, we now need to keep it; but there's no faster way to build trust than to establish a consistent track record of making and delivering upon your commitments. Once you have my trust, not only does it become easier to work together, but I'm also now open to expanding our relationship to a more personal one. Without trust, however, we're trying to build a relationship on an unstable foundation.

Honoring Commitments

Honoring a commitment means that we organize ourselves around seeing that the promise we made is kept. In other words, we do everything within our power to ensure that it happens. In a world of interdependency, however, I often see people struggle with not being able to keep their commitments because someone else in the chain didn't do their part. Is it possible to "honor" a commitment without "keeping" it? Absolutely.

For example, we may have committed to get an answer to a customer by the end of the week, but the supplier hasn't gotten back to us yet. A key component of "honoring" commitments is the ongoing dialogue we have with those to whom we've committed something. We need to do everything possible to see that the commitment is met. However, if circumstances will prevent the timely fulfillment, we have a responsibility to let the other person know at the earliest possible moment, and then to mutually create an alternative. Perhaps a portion of the commitment can be kept, or perhaps a new date can be agreed upon.

People understand that you don't control every facet of delivering upon your promise. However, it's likely that they may be depending on you coming through so that they can, in turn, satisfy commitments they made to others. Unless you notify them of possible changes early, they have no ability to make adjustments on their end. The key is early and frequent communication.

Beware of the "Yes" Man

One of the most frustrating types of people to work with is the well-intentioned person who does so much, but always seems to fall short of keeping his commitments. You know the type. They're usually quick to volunteer for assignments or to say "yes" to anyone's request. You don't want to complain because they're obviously working so hard and because you know they're trying to get it done. It's certainly not for lack of effort. The problem is that you never know when you can count on them.

There's a world of difference between *usually* honoring commitments and *always* honoring commitments. If I usually honor my commitments, and I promise something to you by Tuesday, you don't know for sure whether you can count on it being done. Is this one of the 80% of commitments that I meet, or is this one of the 20% where I fall short? Only if I *always* honor my commitments can you truly rely upon me.

Why We Fall Short

Interestingly, I find that the biggest obstacle to honoring commitments is not the lack of will to get them done. Most of us genuinely want and intend to do what we've promised. No, the most common issue is our sloppiness about the promises or commitments in which we engage. Do these sound familiar?

- A customer asks you to have the product delivered by the end of the month. Not wanting to risk losing the order, you tell them you'll get it done, despite the fact that it's unlikely your supplier can comply with the request.

- A colleague asks you to serve on a planning committee he's put together. It's really important to him, and he knows you'd make a great contribution, but you're already feeling pressure to get your regular work done. You don't want to disappoint him so you agree, knowing that you won't be able to make most of the meetings.

- At the end of your team meeting, assignments are being distributed. You commit to completing the specs for the new system by next Monday, truly expecting to make it happen. However, you also have three other major projects that are due, you'll be away on a family trip on the weekend, and you've promised to attend your daughter's dance recital tomorrow night.

Too often, we promise things that simply cannot be done, given all the other commitments that we also have. It often feels easier to simply say "yes" to another's request, rather than be more rigorous about assessing our ability to fulfill it.

> *I served as a liaison between our clients and our technology vendor. The vendor was notoriously "challenged" with completing their commitments on time. Since this was unacceptable, I had to come up with some practices to ensure that the commitments were kept.*
>
> *First, I would make sure that the commitment was realistic. They tended to blindly commit to a timeframe to complete their tasks without assessing if they could keep the commitment or asking when the client needed the task to be complete. I would ask them about the likelihood of truly completing on time, and if they revealed that it would be a stretch to complete, I'd ask the client if the task could wait a few days. With a rare exception or two, the client was fine with the extra few days when we requested it at the time of commitment. (Waiting until the due date to ask for a few extra days, though, was never a good idea.)*
>
> *I used a task manager tool to track the progress of these projects, setting electronic reminders to make sure they were completed on time. A day or two before the task was due, I would reach out to the vendor to make sure they were on target and, if not, ask what I could do to help. The vendors eventually came to expect these follow-up calls and developed internal practices to make sure the commitments they made to my clients were completed on time. While it took extra effort on my part, keeping everyone accountable for their commitments made a big difference.*
> *-Beth D.*

Another place where our lack of rigor can lead to frustration and misunderstanding is in the language we use around our commitments. I'll bet you've seen these:

- I ask you to get me the report by the end of the day and you reply that you'll "try." Unless I push for more clarification, I don't know what this means. Can I count on having the report or not? I may be relating to it as a commitment while you may not. By the way, not everything has to be a commitment. There can be times where "I'll try" is acceptable, as long as both parties have clarity about what we're saying and what to expect.

- I'm leading a sales team meeting at the end of which I ask everyone to get me their weekly sales reports by the close of business every Monday. When the reports are not all in on time, I get frustrated at my staff's lack of honoring the commitment. But was any commitment made? I simply told them what I wanted. While I still expect compliance, I failed to get any commitment. Though it may seem pedantic, it's quite powerful to go around the room and ask each person to specifically articulate their commitment.

- You call your supplier to solve a billing issue. The person with whom you're dealing says, "I should be able to get that straightened out by tomorrow." Have they made a commitment? No. "I should be able to" is not a commitment. You really don't know what to expect. A commitment includes a specific promised action, a date by which it will be done, and a determination to organize oneself around making it happen.

Notice the relationship between this Fundamental and Fundamental #14 (Set and ask for expectations). Good commitments establish clear expectations for all parties about what is to happen and when. Sloppiness around commitments often leaves people unclear about expectations. Worse yet, it allows two people to have differing sets of expectations. The first step toward honoring our commitments is to increase our discipline about making sure that the commitments we enter into are both clear and realistic.

When I think about those on our staff who truly excelled at honoring commitments, I think mostly about how easy it was to work with them. I'd make a request and they'd either say they could do it, or they couldn't. If they couldn't do it, they'd usually offer a counter-proposal. "I can't commit to having that to you by Tuesday, but would Thursday be OK?" Whatever they committed to, I knew would be accomplished. There's a wonderful simplicity to interactions when we always honor our commitments. Think about how much time and effort is wasted when we're not sure what we can rely upon. Imagine the speed and efficiency that's generated in organizations where honoring commitments is standard operating procedure.

FUNDAMENTAL #22

Be a source for acknowledgement and appreciation.

Positive feedback is a tremendous energy source. Regularly give, receive, and ask for meaningful appreciation and acknowledgement.

Recently, I came across an article about a worldwide survey that was done to examine the most important factors that motivated people to give their best at work. While I wasn't at all surprised to see that "appreciation or recognition for a job well done" was at the top of the list (even before promotions and bonuses), it was nonetheless interesting to ponder the fact that this was a global survey. The recognition that this finding crosses cultural boundaries suggests that there's something innately human about the need to be appreciated. Of course, this certainly matches my own experience, and probably yours as well.

There are few things we can do that are as simple, yet powerful, as providing meaningful acknowledgement and appreciation. When we're acknowledged for work well done, we feel happier, more energized, more positive, and we're more likely to repeat the behavior that generated the acknowledgement. While it's no doubt a simple idea, doing it effectively is a bit more complex.

In my comments that follow, I'll share with you some tips for how to make acknowledgements as impactful as possible, how to avoid the trap of "cheapening" the appreciation you give, and how to appropriately receive acknowledgement. We'll take a look at how to avoid being a "victim" of not getting the type or amount of appreciation you need; and finally, we'll explore how we can even create processes that help us to be more consistent appreciators.

Meaningful Appreciation

Think about a time when you were acknowledged in a way that really "hit home" for you. It probably made your chest swell with pride, and made you feel warm all over. What was it about that particular acknowledgement that made it have so much meaning for you? It's likely that the source of the appreciation had something to do with it. When we're acknowledged by people we respect, people we admire, or people in a position of responsibility, it tends to mean more to us. This is important to keep in mind if you're a leader.

When I was at RSI, I often had to remind myself that simply by being the President, what I said had a different "weight" for many people. Whether I liked it or not, they attached a certain significance to the position of President that carried meaning. Of course, this presented me with many opportunities to appropriately and meaningfully appreciate people.

> *In March, one of my co-workers got married. Our usual practice is to jump in and help when someone is away on vacation (being for each other), so that's what I did, working her book of business while she was out. When she returned, she gave a really nice compliment, letting me know how much she appreciated my thoroughness and how much easier it made it for her to pick right up where she had left off. I didn't feel I did anything more than the normal, though I was recognized as Employee of the Month for my efforts.*
>
> *The impact of her compliment verbally and in writing was HUGE to me. I even still have her acknowledgement at my desk. Because I sat in the corner and was isolated from most others, I usually kept to myself, did my work and went home. Receiving this compliment helped me to break out of my "corner" and help others in my area. I'm also now much better about noticing what others do for me and acknowledging them.*
> *-Mindy J.*

Beyond the source of the acknowledgement, however, there are a number of principles that can help you to make the appreciation you show more meaningful. Let's take a look at a few of those here.

1. Be specific. Tell the other person exactly what you appreciated about what they did. For example, it's far more meaningful to say, "I really appreciate the way you used simple, easy to understand language in your talk today" than to say, "You did a nice job on your talk." Or, "I really appreciate the way you organized the quotes and made the spreadsheet so easy to read. This helped me to more quickly and easily help the client understand their options," rather than, "Nice job on the proposal." The more specific you are, the more clearly the person understands the behavior you're acknowledging and that they should be repeating.

2. Be timely. The closer your acknowledgement is to the event being recognized, the more effective it is for the recipient. It's far more helpful to point out what I did well right after my presentation than two weeks later when I hardly remember it anymore.

3. Describe the impact. Beyond simply noting what was good, describe the impact the acknowledged behavior had. For example, "I really appreciate the way you used simple, easy to understand language in your talk today. This enabled you to connect with the audience better, and it was easy for me to see that they were getting your message clearly." See the difference?

4. Use the appropriate forum. Some people thrive on being recognized in public, especially in front of their peers. For others, though, this is a terrible experience. It unnecessarily makes them feel embarrassed or self-conscious. They much prefer to be acknowledged privately, whether in person or in writing. Know your people and what they value.

The Trap of Cheap Acknowledgement

When my son was in high school, the cross country team, like most school athletic teams, established standards for the achievement of a varsity letter. Being a member of the varsity squad traditionally means that you're in the highest tier of competitors at your school in your given sport. The problem, however, was that in order to give as many people as possible the opportunity to earn a letter, the qualifying standard was set (in my opinion) far too low. While some may think that casting a wider net of inclusion for varsity honors is a good thing, I think it actually has a negative impact.

When we lower our definition of excellence in order to be more inclusive, we hurt everyone. For those who truly achieve at the highest levels, the value of a varsity letter becomes cheapened. For those who barely make the lowered standard and "earn" the letter, they're taught to aim for mediocrity. They don't learn to push themselves to be the best they can be, to stretch their previous beliefs about their limitations.

This same phenomenon has been lamented by many observers of our educational system with regard to so-called "grade inflation." When anyone can easily get an "A," even with minimal performance, it demotivates the best students and gives others a false sense of their achievement.

Insincere acknowledgement has the same effect. If I tell you that you did a wonderful job when you really didn't, I'm doing you no service. For one, it's insincere and it lessens the impact I can have when I really see you do something well. How will you know whether this is a "real" acknowledgement, or whether this is another one of my false platitudes?

For those who really excelled, hearing me say that everyone did a great job is disappointing. Again, it devalues what they accomplished and makes meaningless any genuine appreciation I actually would like to show for them. Perhaps most damaging, this type of "everyone is great" acknowledgement creates a culture of diminished performance. Lowered standards become celebrated as outstanding, and people learn to reduce their expectations. The more sincere your acknowledgment, the greater the power it has to inspire higher performance.

Receiving Acknowledgement

Have you ever noticed how strangely difficult it is to be on the receiving end of meaningful appreciation? We blush, we mumble, we hardly know what to say, we deflect the praise by saying "it really was nothing." While it comes from our own discomfort, think about the impact of denying ourselves the emotional nourishment that a meaningful acknowledgment can provide. Recognize, as well, the impact this has on the one *giving* the acknowledgement. It denies them the full pleasure of their gift to you.

Learn to gracefully accept meaningful appreciation with a simple "thank you." You can even let the other person know that you appreciate that they noticed your contribution, or you can honestly let them know how their acknowledgement makes you feel. Allow yourself to bask in the warmth of a meaningful acknowledgement and let it penetrate your being. When well-deserved, it's a healthy and nourishing feeling—one you need not deflect with false modesty.

No Room for Victims

One of the most common complaints of unhappy workers is the lack of appreciation they feel from their immediate supervisor. In most cases, though, if you ask the worker if they've ever let their supervisor know about this feeling, the answer is usually "no."

To be clear, I'm not at all suggesting that the supervisor shouldn't be paying attention to the needs of his staff. It's one of his most important contributions. I *am* suggesting, though, that supervisors are not mind-readers, and that everyone has a responsibility to "speak straight" about our needs in a way that helps to ensure that those needs are met. While this can feel awkward, if you're not getting what you need, take responsibility to help those around you understand how they can better support you.

Up, Down, and Across the Organization

Sometimes people have a rather hierarchical view of acknowledgement and appreciation, believing that it's mostly limited to managers acknowledging their direct reports. Nothing could be further from the truth. In truly healthy organizations, meaningful appreciation flows freely in all directions: manager to direct report, direct report to manager, and peer to peer.

This was something at which our staff became very good. I frequently witnessed acknowledgement being passed up, down, and across the organization. As we developed a culture where this was expected, people began to notice when others did something worthy of mention. A salesperson might let everyone know how helpful a customer service person was in resolving an issue and the difference it made in us getting the new client. A support person might acknowledge her peers for pitching in to help with a large rush project, allowing it to be completed successfully without anyone having to stay late. This not only feels good to the recipient, but it also serves to reinforce the behavior being acknowledged.

A Structured Approach

In Fundamental #28, I talk at length about the importance of creating systems and processes that support our ability to perform with consistency. And in Fundamental #12, I showed you processes that some great organizations have developed to identify and act upon individualized customer information in order to create a more personal experience. Let me give you some examples of how these same principles can be applied to acknowledgement and appreciation.

At RSI, about every 60 days, I led company-wide staff meetings. It was an opportunity to have everyone together at one time and to connect them to some aspect of our strategy. The second agenda item (the first was the Fundamental of the Week!) was always "Acknowledgements." I would take this opportunity to do 2-4 different meaningful acknowledgements that demonstrated the type of performance I wanted to reinforce. Since I didn't always see all the day-to-day happenings, I would ask my managers to let me know if there was anything in their departments that they thought appropriate for me to acknowledge and then I'd get the details from them. Having this be a regular and expected part of our meeting was a good way of keeping me alert to the good things our people were doing all the time.

Some people are better at keeping alert to these possibilities than others. To help me develop a better habit in this regard, I used the "repeating task" feature in Franklin Planner, my task management software. (For more on task management, see Fundamental #25) I created two tasks that would automatically show up every third day. The first said, "Do personal acknowledgement," and the second said, "Do written acknowledgement." As you can imagine, having to regularly see and complete these tasks was far more helpful to me in staying alert to good opportunities than simply "trying to do a better job."

From a leadership perspective, creating a culture where *meaningful* acknowledgement and appreciation are regular practices can be tremendously empowering. The positive energy literally becomes contagious. From a personal perspective, we all have lots of opportunities to give meaningful appreciation if we're looking for them. Take advantage of those opportunities and watch the difference it makes.

SECTION 4

Personal Effectiveness – These behaviors help us achieve greater personal, and by extension, organizational success.

From paying attention to our appearance, to honing our organizational skills, to learning how to create lasting change, Fundamentals #23 through #30 all describe practices that can make us more effective individuals. When I wrote these Fundamentals, I was thinking about the personal habits that were instrumental in my own success, as well as my experience in observing what made other accomplished people more successful.

While this final group of Fundamentals does have more of a personal focus, its impact on the organization for which you work is equally profound. The more effective we are as individuals, the greater our contributions to our organizations become.

FUNDAMENTAL #23

Take responsibility.

Don't be a "victim." Ask for what you need and take full responsibility for your success.

This is the first of the group of Fundamentals that addresses personal effectiveness, and its position as the first is not by accident. I don't think there's a more foundational principle about effectiveness than this one. All success begins with our acceptance of our own responsibility, for without this, we're left simply waiting for circumstances to serendipitously work out to our advantage.

This notion of responsibility versus victimhood is so critical to understand and accept that I cannot possibly overstate its importance. Everything, and I mean *everything*, we hope to be, achieve, have, or create is rooted in the principle that we take full responsibility for our lives. Think about its opposite for a moment. If we're *not* responsible, then we simply become innocent bystanders in life, passively waiting to see what happens to us. There would be no point in taking any action to improve our lot, since success is out of our hands anyway. While this may seem patently obvious, think about how many people in your circle constantly complain about their job, their boss, their kids, their

— 193 —

spouse, their health, and on and on. When we learn to accept ownership for our circumstances, we spend more time *doing* rather than *complaining*.

Taking responsibility, by the way, does not mean that we can do things alone. We live in an interdependent world in which we must work collaboratively with others to achieve success. Taking responsibility means taking "ownership" for circumstances.

It means asking for what we need, rather than waiting to be given what we need. It means creating the environment we want, rather than depending on others to create it for us or bemoaning the fact that it isn't what we want. It means researching a topic or taking a class, rather than waiting to be taught. It means describing how we want to be treated, rather than complaining that we're not respected. More than anything, taking responsibility is all about recognizing and acting upon our own personal power to create what we want in our lives rather than being a "victim" of circumstance.

To help you get a fuller appreciation for what I mean by taking responsibility, I'm going to examine this notion from nine different perspectives. I'll look at taking responsibility for our

1. Learning
2. Attitudes and emotions
3. Opportunities
4. Health
5. Relationships
6. Actions
7. Results
8. Mistakes
9. Needs

When I'm done, you'll no doubt see why I think this is so important.

Learning

What if I told you that available to nearly every American is virtually all the information you could ever want to learn about almost any topic? What if I told you that access to this information was amazingly simple? And what if I told you that it was all free? Would you believe me? Have you been to your local library recently?

Think about it. In almost every city and town in America, large and small, there is a free public library. And these libraries not only have stacks and stacks of books, magazines, audio recordings, and DVDs on every topic under the sun, but they also subscribe to outside resources that have even more. And it's all free!

To take this one step further, the internet has put virtually unlimited free information in the hands of just about anybody. And if you're one of the few with no computer at home or no internet access, you can almost always get that, too, at your local library.

So here's my question. How can anybody possibly complain that they don't have the skills to improve their situation? Or that they can't afford the learning necessary to achieve their dreams? Or that their company doesn't give them enough training? Or that they're too old to learn the computer? Or that they'd be more employable if they could speak another language?

When we accept responsibility for our own learning instead of waiting for it to be spoon fed to us, whole new worlds open up.

Attitudes and Emotions

Airports can be fascinating places to engage in people watching. Have you ever noticed the wide range of attitudes that emerge when a flight is delayed or cancelled? There will be some people who get all angry and indignant, wondering how the airlines could do this to them, as if they've been somehow singled out for persecution. (OK, I admit, I've allowed myself to feel this way at times, but at least I recognize that feeling that way is a choice I made!) And then there will be other people who, faced with the very same situation, calmly go about making their alternative arrangements.

So what can we conclude from this simple observation? That the circumstances don't determine our attitude; *we* do! We are 100% responsible for choosing whatever attitude we have in any given situation.

When I think of this truth, I always remember an example I heard on an audio cassette program I listened to back in the early '80s. The author was talking specifically about stress. He explained that situations cannot be stressful; in fact, they are completely devoid of emotion. Rather, it's our response to situations that generates stress.

He gave this illustration. Imagine you're on your way to a job interview for a position you've always dreamed about. All of a sudden, traffic comes to a complete stop. No one is moving anywhere, and it's clear this will be a long delay. You have no cell phone and no way of letting anyone know you'll be hours late. Your dream job is rapidly disappearing! Think of how you're feeling as the stress builds. Now, sitting a few cars away, stuck in the same traffic jam is another man. This man has been totally engrossed in an audio book, he's been looking for a chance to listen more, and he has no appointments this afternoon. Think of how he's feeling. One person is stressed; the other is happy. And they're in the same traffic jam! So clearly it's not the traffic jam that's causing the stress. It's the attitude we choose to adopt that's stressful.

And lest we think this only applies to the mundane, we have only to look at an example like Victor Frankl, who wrote <u>Man's Search for Meaning</u> about his experience as a survivor of the Nazi concentration camps. In the face of one of the most horrific situations we can possibly imagine, Frankl famously observed, "Everything can be taken from a man but one thing; the last of the human freedoms—to choose one's attitude in any given set of circumstances, to choose one's own way."

The bestseller <u>Unbroken</u>, by Laura Hillenbrand, is yet another story of how differently people can respond to the most appalling conditions based solely on their chosen attitude. It tells the story of Louis Zamperini, who survived a never-ending series of challenges in Japanese POW camps during World War II while so many of his peers died. Zamperini observed firsthand the remarkable difference each prisoner's attitude made in their ability to withstand horrendous hardships and misfortune.

Think about the inspiring stories we've all heard of people who are paralyzed and choose to live rich, fulfilling lives while others in the same circumstances sink into depression and despair. What's the difference? The attitude they *chose* to have.

While we may recognize that we're, in fact, responsible for our attitudes, many people fail to take the same ownership over their emotions. They'll voice frustration that "she always makes me so angry." Or "my mother makes me feel guilty for not spending enough time with her." Are we just as responsible for these emotions as we are our attitudes?

In the summer before I began college, I read a book that really resonated with me. It was one of Dr. Wayne Dyer's earliest books, <u>Your Erroneous Zones</u>. In one of the early chapters, he talks about this whole issue of owning our emotions, pointing out that ceding control of our emotions to others is abdicating our responsibility to choose how we want to respond to any given situation. He then goes through an exercise where he has the reader rephrase traditional statements into ones that demonstrate ownership. For example, instead of saying, "She always makes me so angry," we change it to, "I always allow myself to get angry by what she does." Or instead of "My mother makes me feel guilty for not spending enough time with her," we learn to say, "I've chosen to feel guilty when I don't spend enough time with my mother." Just this simple change in our language can help us to see that our emotional responses are indeed choices we make, even if we're not always conscious of making them. Taking responsibility means owning our choices, and when we own our choices, the obvious implication is that we can decide to make new choices that serve us better.

Opportunities

Many years ago, we had a guest speaker address the Rotary club I belong to in my hometown of Moorestown, New Jersey. He was a man of about 60 at the time, and he was a very successful businessman. I'll never forget the story he told about coming to America in his late teens or early twenties and being absolutely overwhelmed by the opportunity that existed all around him. What stuck in my mind most though, was not so much how he saw the opportunity and capitalized on it, but his comments about how most Americans are so accustomed to what we have that we don't even recognize the amazing opportunities that surround us. Instead, we too often complain about what we're missing and how no one will give us a chance. Meanwhile, so many people of foreign descent come here to "the land of opportunity," and make their own success. I'm certain that you've seen many examples of this.

To be sure, some people, through nothing but good fortune, are born into situations that make opportunities more readily available to them. The stability of their family, the support and example of their parents, the community they grow up in, the financial resources their family has, all contribute to making the path to success easier. However, history is replete with stories of people who've squandered these advantages and stories of other people who chose to take responsibility for their lives and created success with the most meager of apparent opportunities.

I remember reading Richard Wright's autobiography, Black Boy, in high school. If you've never read it, I highly recommend it. The obstacles he overcame to learn to read and write, let alone to become a well-educated man and fabulous author, are almost impossible to believe. And there are countless more stories just like his. That's not to suggest that it's easy or even common, because it's not. The odds are clearly heavily stacked in favor of some and against others. But the fact remains, we're all responsible for the choices we make in how we live our lives. Some recognize and accept that responsibility, while others choose to wallow in the misery of being helpless victims.

Health

Before I address what it looks like to take responsibility for our health, let me say that I fully recognize sometimes we suffer from conditions for no reason other than bad luck. It's tragic when a child is born with a serious health condition, or an adult is suddenly stricken with a debilitating disease. These are not choices (though our responses to these challenges certainly *are* choices).

However, outside of these types of terrible situations, how often do we fail to take ownership over our health? "I used to exercise more, but I have bad knees." "I know I should lose weight, but I can't seem to find a diet that works for me." We do have control over what we eat, how much we sleep, how much we exercise, whether we smoke, how much we drink, whether we take drugs, and more.

I also want to be clear that I'm not advocating any type of regimen at all here. I'm simply wanting us to own our choices. The essence of this Fundamental is recognizing that we are responsible for what happens in our lives. With few exceptions, if our health is good, we're responsible; and if our health is poor, we're responsible.

Relationships

Think about every relationship you have or have ever had that's been less than you want or wanted it to be. What's the one common denominator in every one of these circumstances? You! That's not to suggest that you're the cause of the dissatisfaction since all relationships, by definition, involve more than one person. Rather, I want to point out that since you're a part of it you can either wait for someone else to change or you can take responsibility for moving the relationship closer to what you want it to be.

Lloyd Fickett, the developer of The Collaborative Way, used to say about listening that, "If someone's not listening to you, ask yourself what you're not hearing from them." I think the same is true about our relationships. If they're not what we want them to be, a good starting point is to at least consider what role we play in the dynamic, and what opportunities we may have for positive change. Are you waiting for others, or are you taking responsibility?

> *Though misunderstandings between people happen often, I find that when I'm willing to take responsibility for "cleaning it up," I can make the relationship even stronger. One day, I learned that a coworker was upset with me because she felt that I was ignoring her. I couldn't imagine how she had come to that conclusion, so to me, the only option was to go and talk with her—to take responsibility for myself, and for our relationship, to try to understand and repair.*
>
> *When I approached her to learn more, she shared her perception that I was ignoring her when I passed her in the hallways; these situations were those where she was in a small group and having a conversation. To me, to say hello was to interrupt—that's rude! But to her, saying hi, even when another conversation was going on— that was friendly. So I apologized and worked to acknowledge her anytime I passed her. These efforts went a long way to making our working relationship a positive one.*
> *-Sharyn S.*

Actions

How many times have you read stories about a child who gets in trouble at school for some misdeed and his parents go to the administration or the teacher claiming, "My little Johnny couldn't be at fault?" What lesson does the child learn about taking responsibility and the relationship between actions and consequences?

How many times have you read or heard stories about someone who falls off a balcony in a drunken stupor and then sues the building owner for not having a secure enough railing? Most of the stories we hear are of people seeing themselves as victims, not responsible for their actions. I touched on this a bit in Fundamental #6 – Practice blameless problem solving. We've created a mentality where many people spend more time figuring out who they can blame for their misfortune than they do taking responsibility for their choices. All positive change begins with us owning responsibility for our actions.

Results

I once heard Ron Williams, the former Chairman and CEO of Aetna, say "We appreciate effort, but we reward results." I've always found that to be a particularly insightful statement, for many people confuse the two. When I'd ask one of our staff whether we got the client their answer, I'd sometimes hear about how many messages were left for our insurance carrier contact over how many days, or I'd hear about all the different people we tried to reach. But, in the end, the client really doesn't care. They just want their answer.

Taking responsibility for results means doing whatever is necessary to achieve the objective. Allowing ourselves to be thwarted in our attempts to solve a problem, or be satisfied with simply having tried, is just another form of victimhood. It's saying, "The world didn't give me what I wanted" rather than taking ownership for making it happen.

I used to play a hypothetical game with myself that helped me to discern whether or not I was really taking responsibility for results or just blaming circumstances and playing the role of victim. I called it the "million dollar game," and it went like this: Suppose I needed to reach someone to solve a problem and I had tried every way I could think of with no success. I'd ask myself, "If someone were to offer me $1 million if I could reach this person today, would I be able to think of a way to do it?" You bet I could! I could come up with lots of "out of the box" approaches to reach the person, if the stakes were high enough.

It's amazing how much more creative we can become when sufficiently motivated. My point here isn't that we should always go to those lengths. Rather, my point is for us to be honest in taking responsibility for our results. I'd rather say that I've made a choice about how far I'm willing to go in pursuit of achieving a result, than to accept my lack of results as a victim, believing it was not possible to achieve more.

Mistakes

In Fundamental #2, I gave examples of five behaviors that were indicative of checking the ego at the door, one of which was the ability to admit a mistake and change direction. This is also an indication of your ability to take responsibility. Rather than wasting time blaming others (see Fundamental #6), the sooner we own our mistakes, the faster we can move on to correcting them.

A good practice for developing this ability is to learn to ask yourself, "In what way, if at all, might I have contributed to this mistake?" Particularly if you're a leader, you might consider whether you provided enough direction, resources, clarity, and training for the job to be completed successfully. Taking responsibility for mistakes also helps to win the loyalty and respect of those who report to you.

Even if you're not a leader, the same question can also be enlightening. Before you play victim and assume the problem is elsewhere, do an honest assessment of any role you may have played—and own it.

> *I recently had a dispute with my contact in our home office over the correct procedures to use for entering certain statements. Frustrated, I wrote her an e-mail, copying her boss, asking for someone to explain to her the way we had been directed to complete the forms. She immediately got upset, became defensive, and involved my boss. When he pointed out that the tone of my e-mail made it sound like my contact was incompetent, I was mortified.*
>
> *The more I thought about it, the more I could see how she might have perceived it—e-mails don't always come across the way they're intended. I decided I better check my ego at the door and take responsibility for this miscommunication. I called her and apologized and asked her if we could start over from this point. She was so glad I called and, since then, our relationship has become better than ever.*
>
> *I find that I rely on using the Fundamentals as I interact with others in both my professional and personal life. At first, it took practice, but over time, they've become a part of me. Even my family has noticed the huge difference, and they, in turn, are beginning to use these Fundamentals with those they come into contact with.*
> *-Denise L.*

Needs

One of the most common situations in which I see people act like victims is when it comes to having their needs met, as if the world should somehow anticipate what they need and supply it to them. For example, I'll hear someone complain that no one taught them how to do a particular job. Or they'll complain that they weren't getting enough feedback. If you're not getting enough feedback, it's your responsibility to let your supervisor know that you need more. To be clear, I'm not suggesting here that managers should wait around for their reports to ask for feedback. What I *am* suggesting is that if you're not getting what you need, acting like a victim is not acceptable.

Another book I'd recommend on this topic is a fascinating work I read by Jack Canfield and Mark Victor Hansen called <u>The Aladdin Factor</u>. The premise of the book is that amazing things are available to us if we will only ask. The authors look at the reasons we're typically reluctant to ask for what we want, and they relate numerous stories of people who've done incredible things simply because they weren't afraid to ask. Where some play the victim, others take responsibility and ask for what they want.

One final example of the impact of taking responsibility for our needs is the discussion I had in Fundamental #2). Remember not to be a victim about not getting the right kind or amount of appreciation. Take responsibility and let others know what you need.

I've mentioned throughout this book my experience that most people either already come to work with many of the attributes I've been discussing or they don't, and the propensity to take responsibility for their lives is no exception. If you listen to the way people speak, and the stories they tell, it reveals much about how they view this issue.

Victims tend to talk about their misfortunes in terms of how the world has conspired against them: their last boss was stupid; their teacher failed them; their coach played favorites. They never seem to understand the role they play in their successes and failures.

People who take responsibility, however, tend to be doers and learners. They make things happen. And when circumstances don't work out the way they want, they first look at themselves to see what they can learn and what they can do differently to create a different outcome the next time.

Here's one of my favorite quotes on this topic. It was written by a man named Michael Gerber, who wrote the book The E-myth Revisited. He said,

> The difference between great people and everyone else is that great people create their lives actively, while everyone else is created by their lives, passively waiting to see where life takes them next. The difference between the two is the difference between living fully and just existing.

Accepting responsibility for what happens in our lives is the foundation on which success is built. Take responsibility and create what you want in your life.

FUNDAMENTAL #24

Appearance counts.

Your personal appearance makes a strong statement about the pride you take in your performance. Dress neatly and professionally. The appearance of our office makes a similar statement about the quality of our work. Take responsibility to see that our office environment is clean, neat, and professional.

Have you ever noticed how quickly we judge people based on their appearance? We see someone coming toward us with spiked purple hair, multiple tattoos, and a variety of body piercings, and we immediately form our opinions. To be sure, we really know nothing about them, but we quickly draw inferences about a whole host of characteristics based solely on their appearance. We may make assumptions about their intelligence, their work ethic, their work quality, their value system, and even whether or not we like them; and truth be told, we're only guessing about it all. And then we relate to our conclusions as if they're fact, even when we have such limited data.

The reason I point this out is not to comment on whether we *should* or *should not* judge with such haste. Rather it's to point out that we *do*. And we *all* do it. Whether we like it or not and whether we should or not, we form opinions about people, and they about us, based largely on appearance. So, if this is true, it makes sense to at least pay attention to our appearance so that we project the image that we want.

Let me give you another example that's not so exaggerated. Imagine that you're interviewing two CPAs to select someone to handle your taxes. The first one is dressed in a nicely tailored suit and tie, with shoes shined, and works in an office that appears neat and orderly. The second one is sloppily dressed with a wrinkled suit, scuffed shoes, crooked tie, and his shirttail hanging out, and works in an office with piles of papers and file folders strewn about. Which one inspires more confidence? While there are obviously far more important qualities necessary to being a great CPA than the way you dress, your appearance nevertheless *does* send a strong message about your approach.

When you pay attention to the details of your appearance, you tell the world that you're likely to pay attention to the details of your work. It's tremendously difficult to be sloppy in some areas of our lives—particularly the most visible ones—and then miraculously become meticulous and detailed in other areas.

The Military Gets It

Have you ever considered why the military is so famously fanatical about how they wear their uniform? Think about the image of a Marine in full dress uniform. What do you picture? The uniform is absolutely crisp and it's spotless. I picture the shoes being so shiny you can see your reflection. Even the buttons on the uniform jacket are polished to a brilliant shine. And think of the posture of a Marine at attention. No slumping there!

Every branch of the military is equally rigorous about these details. They inspect and inspect and inspect, and demand nothing less than perfection. Why?

Because the military understands that when we take pride in our appearance, that pride carries over into other areas of our lives. And when we're sloppy in our appearance, that carries over as well. In preparing for potential battle, there's no room for shortcuts, sloppiness, and poor quality.

Dress Codes Vary

When we think of the work setting, there's no doubt that societal norms have changed with regard to what's considered professional or appropriate. Fewer and fewer people are wearing formal business suits, and business casual has become the norm. Indeed "Casual Friday" has morphed into casual every day. And, of course, there are also places we now see where the dress code might best be described as "anything goes."

The dress code for a business should be appropriate for its industry and for the culture in which it operates. What's suitable for a business consultant will certainly be different from what's suitable for a graphic designer. And what's considered to be appropriate in Thailand may be different from what's expected in the United States. However, whatever *is* worn can and should be worn neatly.

We've all seen people dressed in business casual attire, and even jeans, who look quite sharp. They pay attention to looking neat no matter what they wear. And we've all seen people wear suits who look like total slobs. They could wear a tuxedo and look like a mess. So this isn't so much about what's the appropriate dress code as it is about how you present yourself.

There's a distinction that I think is important here about appearance for others and appearance for ourselves. Since people will judge us based on our appearance, it's important to understand the expectations of our industry and our customers and to be conscious of projecting the image that we want to portray.

But as my example of the military points out, I also find that our appearance has a direct bearing on our self-image, and our self-image has a direct bearing on our performance. Try this simple experiment. Put this book down for a moment and walk around the room standing tall and straight, shoulders back, stomach pulled in tight. How do you feel? Now walk around the room with slumped shoulders, stomach out, slouching. Do you notice the difference? Most of us literally feel different when we stand tall. We carry ourselves differently and we feel more self-confident. And there's no doubt that how we feel about ourselves impacts how we perform. If it didn't, the military wouldn't be so emphatic about their standards.

An Orderly Work Environment

This same principle applies to our workspace and to our overall work environment. When a visiting prospect or a customer walks past your desk and sees piles of papers and files strewn over your entire work area with seemingly no order, how do you think this affects their confidence that you'll effectively juggle and manage all the important details of their job? Conversely, when they see a neat, clean, well-organized work area, it increases their confidence in your individual ability as well as that of the organization as a whole. If we're meticulous about the details of our environment, we're more likely to be meticulous about the details of our work.

Let me stop for just a moment here to issue a disclaimer. Undoubtedly, we can all think of some exception to what I've put forth here. We all know some person who looks like a total mess, keeps their work area in shambles, and somehow manages to produce good work on time without missing assignments. But I will tell you from my experience, and I'm certain your experience will bear this out, that 9 out of 10 workers who look like I just described will perform at a level far below that of which they're capable.

For most of our clients at RSI, the decision-making contact was usually the CFO. I always found it fascinating to visit these CFOs in their offices. With a high degree of consistency, those CFOs whose offices were neat and orderly seemed to dress the same way, and they were usually on top of the details of their companies. Those whose offices were piled with file folders on the desk, on the floor, and even on their window sills, usually dressed sloppily, constantly missed deadlines, and often struggled to deliver on the commitments they made.

At RSI, it was important for us to keep our office neat, clean, and orderly. We encouraged prospects to do site visits to get a better sense for who we were and

Two years ago, I had a prospect come to our office for a site visit. We gave them the usual tour, which included seeing how the office functioned, meeting the people, sitting for a software demo, and getting a feel for our culture. When they left, they were so impressed that they said they couldn't imagine choosing any other organization. Of course, as sometimes happens, they were then wooed by a promise made by another broker, and went with him.

Three months ago, they called me back. Things didn't work out with the other broker and now they realized their mistake. They told me that they couldn't get over the feeling they had from visiting us. The office was so well organized, the processes were so clearly defined, and the people were so friendly. Everything they saw told them that RSI was different, and this time, we were the only ones they called. I'm happy to say they're now a happy client.
-Dennis B.

the way in which we worked. Since a big part of choosing an advisor is trust and confidence, it was important for them to get a feel for the organization. We wanted our environment to inspire our visitors to feel confidence in us. We wanted them to know that we would be on top of every detail of their plans, and that we had the kinds of systems and processes in place that exemplified high quality. It was important for our office environment to be consistent with every other part of what they perceived to be the RSI experience.

Shared Responsibility

By the way, when it comes to maintaining a neat and clean office, everyone must take responsibility (see Fundamental #23). It's amazing to see how many times people will walk by a piece of trash on the floor in the hallway without picking it up, assuming it must be someone else's job. An office is a community, and everyone has to play a role in maintaining it. Since every person grew up in a different type of household with different expectations and habits around cleanliness, it's essential that the leadership establishes the standards for cleanliness and organization as a part of the organizational culture. Unless this is defined clearly and then reinforced, it will always sink back to the lowest common denominator.

It's been said that you only get one chance to make a good first impression. Make sure that the first one you make is truly the one you want to project. Reaffirm that impression continually by paying attention to your personal appearance and the appearance of your work environment.

FUNDAMENTAL #25

Being organized makes a difference.

Maintain a clean and orderly work area. Use an effective task management system to keep track of outstanding issues and responsibilities. Maintain an orderly filing system.

In a work world of interdependence, we're constantly making promises to others and having others make promises to us. We're juggling multiple tasks and managing a variety of issues at the same time. What could be more important to our success than having good systems for keeping track of everything that's "on our plate?"

You Have It or You Don't

Like so many of the values I've described throughout this book, my experience has shown me that most people come to the workplace with their orientation toward organization already formed. In other words, either they're organized or they're not. Someone who's well-organized usually prefers orderliness to chaos. The systems they use to create order in their lives may be fairly unsophisticated or they may be highly refined, but they generally work adequately well for that person. I can take someone who is oriented toward organization and give them new tools to be even more effective; but almost never can I take a disorganized person and make them organized, no matter how good the tools may be.

This lesson has been driven home for me many times during my career. I can think of one consultant, in particular, that we hired who was the poster child for why this Fundamental is so important. He was a very bright man, an outstanding consultant with a great deal of experience. His ability to understand complex issues and give quality advice to clients was unquestioned. However, he was terribly disorganized; and the result of this flaw was that he couldn't effectively handle multiple issues and commitments and see that everything was accomplished on time. If he only had to work with one or two clients, he would be exceptional; but the economic reality was that in order to justify his salary he needed to be able to manage a "book" of business that included at least 15-20 clients.

We tried every way we could think of to help him, including providing additional administrative support, yet nothing worked. While a great administrative assistant can make an executive look better, if the person isn't generally oriented toward being well-organized, their success becomes highly limited. In this case, that weakness held back an otherwise promising career.

One interesting note about this predisposition to orderliness is that it's unclear at what age it typically develops, or at what age you can be sure it's simply never going to happen. Growing up, my son never showed signs of being particularly organized. Once he started college, however, he developed a real appreciation for its importance and now thrives on developing good systems that help him to keep organized and to manage his many responsibilities. Here again, I can provide him with additional tools to help him improve his effectiveness, but I can't provide the desire or appreciation for being organized in the first place. That has to come from within.

People who are better organized accomplish more work, in less time with fewer mistakes and with less stress, than their counterparts who are not as well organized. At RSI, this issue was important enough that for many years I actually taught classes for our staff on a system I developed over time for effectively managing our work. It's a 5-part system, outlined as follows, that I still use today.

The 5-Part System

Here are the elements that I've found, when combined, can make a significant difference in effectiveness.

1. A clean desk. Managing our work begins with managing our work area. An orderly work area allows us to maintain greater focus amidst what can sometimes feel like chaos. While I've heard some people claim to work well in chaos, insisting they "know where everything is," I would strongly contend that each of us could be more effective if our surroundings were more orderly.

Besides time wasted trying to locate things, the real issue with a messy desk is distraction. When there are piles of papers strewn all over our desk, each time we reach for the phone or for a file, our eyes momentarily see another piece of paper and our minds briefly shift focus to register that paper. It's like creating for ourselves a constant source of interruption. When our desk is clear however, we can more easily focus our attention on one thing at a time.

2. A "to sort" tray. A "to sort" tray is a place on our desk where all incoming items are temporarily placed until we move them to their appropriate place. It's similar to a traditional "in" box, but items move out of it much more quickly. In boxes typically end up being a repository of papers and files that never seem to diminish. In contrast, items are only in the "to sort" tray for less than one day. In a moment, I'll show you how this works in concert with the other elements to create an effective system.

By the way, the other value of a "to sort" tray is that it focuses all incoming items in one place. Without this, other people will tend to place things all over our desks just so that they can make sure we see them. Of course, that just adds to the chaos.

3. A work pending or suspense file. Every good system should have some place (off the desk) for putting work that we're waiting to work on. I used a "work pending" file that I kept in an easily accessible drawer. Others prefer to have suspense systems organized by date or by topic. The key is that papers and files associated with issues we're not working with right this minute should be put away out of sight, but in a place we where we can easily get to them.

4. A "waiting for return call" file. I often found that I would be working on an issue and would have to leave a message for someone before being able to resolve it. When the person called me back, I wanted to be able to quickly pick up the associated paperwork, but didn't want to leave it on my desk to become a distraction. The "waiting for a return call" file solved this problem. It was a file in my top drawer where I put only those things associated with calls I was waiting for. This got it off my desk, but still kept it accessible.

5. A task management system. A good task management system is far more than a list of things to do. It's a system that allows us to assign tasks to the specific times they should be done, allows us to prioritize tasks, and allows us to keep track of things that haven't yet been completed. These systems can be in paper, like DayTimers, Franklin Planner, and others; or they can be electronic, like Outlook, Franklin Planner, Act!, Goldmine, and many others. I was particularly partial to Franklin Planner, produced by FranklinCovey.

Let me demonstrate how these elements work together. Every job that needs to be done is listed in the task management program for the appropriate day, and is prioritized. As a new item hits the "to sort" tray, I determine when it should be worked on, add it to the task list for the appropriate day, and put the paperwork away in the appropriate suspense file. When it's time to work on an issue, I pull it from the appropriate place. If I need to wait for an answer, it goes in the "waiting for a return call" file. In this way, I can stay as focused as possible on each task as I work on it.

By the way, when you examine why people have papers and files all over their desk, there are usually two major reasons. One: they don't want to forget to do something, and having the file in front of them serves as a reminder. And two: they want to be able to get to it quickly when they need it.

Notice how a good system like I've outlined easily eliminates both reasons. If we enter all tasks in our planning system, we are never at risk of forgetting anything. And if we put things away in our "work pending" or "waiting for a return call" file, we can get them at a moment's notice. There really is no good reason to allow the distractions that are caused by a cluttered work area.

Common Complaints

Sometimes I'll hear people complain that they start their day intending to be well-organized, but then surprises happen and it throws them off their plan. My response is that unforeseen issues don't mean we stop planning and being organized; rather, we constantly adjust our plan based on smart prioritization. When the new issue arises, we add it to our task list, determine its priority, and then continue to work issues in priority order. The fact that it's in our face does not mean that it's the highest priority item. A good system will always allow us to make intelligent choices about what we should be working on, rather than simply working on whatever we see first. Prioritization is one of the biggest keys to effectiveness.

> In my job as a consultant, I'm responsible for handing all the insurance renewal activity for more than 30 clients. I use a weekly list of "things to do" as well as a grid of the renewals by client and line of coverage that encompasses the next 150 days and the previous 60 days. Here's how it works:
>
> I meet with my support team typically every Wednesday morning. We review the list of things to do and we all agree on who is going to do what. The grid has been set up to look back 60 days to ensure that all renewal tasks have been handled for each line of coverage and that the database and file have been updated. The portion of the grid that encompasses the next 150 days allows us to plan for upcoming renewals, prioritize our workload, and proactively reach out to the carriers to begin setting expectations for the release of the renewals. Staying organized allows me to keep my sanity while making sure everything gets done on time.
> -Jeff O.

Another complaint I would often hear is that "I'm too busy to get organized. I'll clean up when I have a free moment to catch my breath." There is absolutely no doubt in my mind that, no matter how busy we are, taking time to get organized first saves many multiples of that time moving forward, not to mention reduces errors, lowers stress, and increases quality.

Incidentally, none of us is perfect at maintaining our systems. Sometimes we let things slide a little and we then periodically have to "clean up." For example, I was not always as disciplined as I'd like to be about keeping my "work pending" file pure in terms of only keeping things I'm about to work on. Sometimes it would tend to become a bit of a miscellaneous catch all. To help me with this, I would create a task to clean my work pending file every Friday. In this way, I kept it from getting out of hand.

The same principle works well with your desk. If you find that your desk starts to get messier than you'd like, despite your best efforts at maintaining a clear work area, then at least clean it up once each week. This is far better than simply giving up and working amidst chaos and clutter.

There are as many different systems for keeping organized as there are people, and no one system is right for everyone. However, all effective systems must enable you to

- Keep track of what needs to be accomplished and when,
- Prioritize tasks by importance,
- Find what you need quickly and easily, and
- Focus your attention with minimal distraction.

Stress Reduction

Have you ever had one of those Saturdays where you felt almost overwhelmed because you were thinking of all the different tasks around the house you wanted to get done as well as all the errands you needed to do? Have you noticed what happens when you start the day by getting them all out of your head and making a list where you can cross off items as they're completed?

Just the simple act of getting the tasks organized so that we can see them gives us a sense of control; and as we feel more in control, we feel more productive and less stressed. The same thing happens at work. The more we feel in control of what needs to be accomplished, the less overwhelmed we feel and the more productive we become.

The link between being better organized and being more effective is unequivocal. Any time you spend improving your personal organization is paid back many times over. Invest the time.

FUNDAMENTAL #26

Double-check all work.

Proofread all letters, e-mails, spreadsheets, etc. for accuracy and correctness. Accuracy is a reflection of A+ness.

This one of the simplest Fundimentals to do, has one of the biggest paybacks in terms of quality, and yet is oneof the most frequently overlooked. Notice anything wrong with that sentence?

You should see three glaring errors, only two of which will even be picked up by spellcheck or grammar check. The third error is a missing word that you'll only notice if you proofread carefully. What would you think if this book was filled with these types of errors? What statement would it make about me (and perhaps even the publisher)? How would it affect my credibility? How might it affect the likelihood of you doing business with me?

It's shocking to see how many printed documents—letters, signs, posters, even billboards—have blatant errors in them. Things like confusing "its" with "it's" or "there" with "their." There's really no excuse, since these types of errors can so easily be avoided by careful proofreading.

Errors that could have been eliminated by proofreading are a sign of sloppiness; and if I'm sloppy in what I present to you, it's likely to be indicative of a general inattention to detail. Is that the kind of person or organization you want to be, or want to work with?

The place I typically see the most errors is in e-mail. Perhaps because it tends to be such a quick and informal type of communication, most people don't bother checking over their work. While I don't like it, I can understand this laziness when it's an informal message between friends or family members. But when we're communicating with the outside world, and especially with customers, there's no room for words being misspelled or sentences that are missing words. Spellcheck is an easy tool to use to catch many errors, but it won't catch missing words or words used incorrectly. Before you hit the "send" button, take the extra time (Fundamental #4) to read over what you've written to be certain it's of a quality that you can be proud of.

Spreadsheet Errors

Spreadsheets are an easy place for errors to happen. Because the formulas are hidden behind the cells, it's not always obvious when a mistake exists. Especially in a large spreadsheet with many pages and loads of entries, how do you notice when something doesn't look right? There are two ways that I've learned to catch such errors.

The first way is to spot check different cells to be sure that the answer matches what you would expect to see. The key here is using your estimating skills. For example, if a cell was to calculate the total sales volume and my team had sold 103 units @ $52 per unit, I would expect the answer to be somewhere in the neighborhood of $5,000. If my answer, however, showed a number closer to $50,000 it would tell me that I must have made a mistake in my formula. If commission payments were 10% of sales, then I should expect to see total commissions paid in the range of $500. Any number vastly different from this would again reveal a hidden error somewhere. I look all around my spreadsheets and check different calculations to be sure they're at least in the ballpark of what I might expect to see through estimating.

I remember when my children were in middle school, they did a unit on estimating in math. They practiced being able to determine *approximately* what an answer should be. This is truly a relevant skill in double-checking our work. If you know around what the result should be, then you can more easily spot numbers that look fishy.

The second way to check for errors is to do some opposite calculations. Multiplication is a good way to check your division, and addition is a good way to check your subtraction. When I was in high school, I had a particularly demanding math teacher who always required us to show the "check" we did for every problem. In other words, after we solved the problem, we had to write out the opposite equations we used to confirm that our answer was correct. In fact, if we didn't show the check, she deducted points from our work! I learned this valuable habit back then and still use it today.

When we're working on a big spreadsheet, we often do lots of cutting and pasting of formulas to save us from having to repeat laborious entries. While this is undoubtedly the most effective way to accomplish the goal, it's also replete with opportunities for errors. Something as simple as whether or not a portion of a formula should be held "constant" when being pasted to another area of the spreadsheet can make all the difference in the world. The more complex the spreadsheet, the more likely it is that there will be an error. I almost always have mistakes in my spreadsheets on the first try. Double- and triple-checking helps me to catch those errors before my work is done.

Templates

Here's a place where it's wise to be extra careful: using previously created templates. Let me give you an example. Suppose you're preparing a presentation for Client B that's similar to one you already did for Client A. Rather than starting everything from scratch for Client B, you use the template you prepared for Client A, and then just change the name of the company and a few details that are specific to Client B. Too many times, I've seen this done where the name was changed on all of the pages except for one. Or there's one page accidentally left in the presentation that doesn't really apply to Client B. These can be embarrassing oversights when they come to light in front of the client. Be on the lookout for this type of error and pay extra attention when using previously created templates.

A Few Proofreading Tips

Here are a few proofreading tips based on my experience:

1. **Take a break**. Sometimes we're too close to what we've written and we can't easily see our mistakes. It can help to take a break and then look at our work with a fresh pair of eyes.

2. **Read in reverse order**. Another way of getting a fresh perspective is to read what you've written in reverse order, from bottom to top. By breaking the usual pattern, we make it less likely that our brains automatically pro-

cess what we see as what we *expect* to see, and not what's actually there.

3. **Have someone else review**. Here again, sometimes we're so sure of what we expect to read (because we wrote it), that we don't notice the errors that are right in front of us. Having someone else proofread for us can often turn up mistakes we hadn't detected.

4. **Print a hard copy**. I often find that my eyes don't pick up on everything as easily when I'm reviewing copy on the computer. Printing my document makes it easier for me to examine it critically and find anything that doesn't look right.

More than many, this Fundamental requires discipline. I've heard it said that "the price of excellence is eternal vigilance." Remember that when you produce a document, whether it's an e-mail, a proposal, a report, a spreadsheet, or any other work product, it represents you. Take pride in the quality of your work. Be certain that it's worthy of your signature. The path to high quality is simple: proofread, proofread, and proofread.

FUNDAMENTAL #27

Look ahead and anticipate.

Be prepared by anticipating future needs and addressing them today. Avoid mistakes that come with last-minute actions.

When I look at mistakes that are made, it's startling to see how many of them are the result of rushing to complete work at the last minute. In our haste, we inevitably fail to catch an error or to double-check our work (see Fundamental #26). Or, we forget to include something important and are unprepared. And when I dig deeper, it's equally startling to see how often these mistakes are avoidable if we look ahead and anticipate rather than waiting until that last minute.

This Fundamental is one of the most simple, yet powerful methods I know of to reduce stress and increase effectiveness. Perhaps the fact that it's so simple is why it's so often overlooked, yet learning to do this one thing pays enormous dividends in so many ways. Let's take a look at a few different types of anticipation, and examine more closely the impact they can have.

1. Anticipate your schedule. As you plan your day, be sure to look at your schedule for next week and next month. What's coming up that needs preparation in advance? What answers might you need before you even begin working? Are there opportunities to be requesting those answers now so that you have them when you need them? Are there supplies or other resources you might need? What might go wrong at the last minute that you can anticipate now and possibly prevent?

Here's a simple example: You have a meeting with a client 10 days from now. In order to prepare your presentation, you'll need certain proposals and you'll need time to review those proposals for additional questions. By planning in advance, you can make sure that the proposals are in on time and that you have sufficient time to get answers to any relevant questions in the proposal prior to meeting with the client. In contrast, if you wait until the appointment is the next day, you may not have the correct or complete information. By the time you discover this, it's too late. You rush off to the client feeling stressed and overwhelmed, racing around for the missing pieces, and increasing the risk of errors that you didn't have time to check. And it can all be avoided by looking ahead.

2. Anticipate questions. This is not so much about reducing errors as it is about increasing effectiveness. As you plan for a meeting, learn to anticipate the questions that others may have. This enables you to do any necessary research in advance and come to the meeting more fully prepared. It increases the confidence others have in you and it saves significant time.

In Fundamental #22 I mentioned the entire staff meetings I used to conduct to keep our organization aligned around our strategy and plans. Whenever I was intending to roll out a significant initiative, I would anticipate the questions people might have and prepare, in advance, a written Q&A document, organized by topic, to distribute following the meeting. This not only gave them the information they needed, but it also gave them a sense of confidence that my plans were thorough and well thought-out.

By the way, to do this effectively, you need to practice thinking from the perspective of others. If you were in their shoes, what questions might you have? What might be your concerns? The better you are at seeing the issue from another viewpoint, the better prepared you can be to answer the inevitable questions.

3. Anticipate counter-arguments. Another form of anticipating questions is to anticipate counter-arguments or objections. This is valuable in meetings as well as in our writing. If you're making a sales call, anticipating what objections the prospect might have allows you the chance to be prepared with useful responses. If you're explaining a proposed initiative to your staff, anticipating their objections allows you to come better prepared with whatever information might be helpful to enable them to align.

This process is just as important in our writing. One of the things I try to do in my writing is to anticipate where the reader may disagree or may have a counter-argument to the point I'm making. I then try to raise that issue myself and respond to it. I'm trying to stay one step ahead and demonstrate that I've thought about this idea from various angles.

4. Anticipate needs. When you look at your schedule and see what you have coming up, it's helpful to ask yourself what resources you may need to accomplish your tasks or to prepare for your meetings. There's nothing like starting to put that big presentation together and discovering at the last minute that you don't have the specialized paper you need or that someone else has reserved the projector for the same time. If you know this far enough in advance, you can find a way around the problem;

but if you don't realize it until the last minute, you're scrambling around like crazy trying to avoid a disaster. And it can almost always be avoided by looking ahead and anticipating your needs.

5. Anticipate problems. While this may sound negative, as if we're expecting things to go wrong, I don't mean it that way. Rather, what I'm suggesting is that you take the time to imagine what could possibly go wrong, and have some contingency plan for how you might address it if it occurs. In fact, some refer to this as "contingency planning." The extreme version of this is disaster recovery planning. Anticipating what kind of disasters could happen and how you might deal with them is an important part of being a well-run organization. It helps to ensure continuity in the event of an emergency.

Well short of disasters, however, there are plenty of situations in which it's useful to imagine what might go wrong and to plan for either prevention or remediation. For many years, my brother and I would have a weekly conversation about where we thought our biggest vulnerability was as an organization. This was also part of our management team's semi-annual strategic planning. Having this discussion increased our awareness of potential breakdowns and helped us to take steps to reduce their likelihood.

Some people might complain that they're just so swamped putting out fires and taking care of today's issues that they don't have an opportunity to look further ahead. (Notice the anticipation of a counter-argument?) To me, this is a bit like the person who complains that they don't have time to plan their day (see Fundamental #25). Just as taking 10 minutes at the beginning of each day to organize yourself and prioritize your plans saves you hours in unproductive effort, the same is true with regard to anticipating. Taking just a few minutes to look ahead at your schedule and anticipate future requirements allows you to make better choices to manage your time more effectively. The result is being more productive, more effective, more accurate, and less stressed.

Develop the habit of looking ahead and planning your work accordingly.

> Last summer, I was asked to give administrative support to our regional director while his assistant took a short term leave of absence. I had an upfront conversation with him about his expectations, and then followed that up with a conversation with his current assistant. We went over the responsibilities I would cover while she was out, and how the director preferred certain things be done. Everything was set to hand over the reins to me.
>
> As I was preparing myself to take over the new tasks, I started thinking ahead about any issues I may have, so that I could resolve them before the assistant went out on leave. That's when I realized I wasn't on the same system that they were! My office uses Outlook and the director and his assistant were both on Lotus Notes. There was no way I could access his calendar and emails and expense reports without being set up on these systems by our IT Department. I quickly reached out to the appropriate people to make this happen. If I hadn't thought ahead and realized this pretty big issue, the director would have been left without an assistant who could access his calendar for a few days, resulting in possibly missed meetings or embarrassing scheduling conflicts.
> -Winnie D.

FUNDAMENTAL #28

Have a bias for structure and rebar.

Look to create systems and processes that support our ability to perform with consistency.

Have you ever noticed the way in which concrete is installed in a major road construction project, perhaps one that includes bridges and overpasses? Steel rods are often used as a means of reinforcement or support, and then the concrete is poured around them. These rods are known as "rebar." In a similar way, we can create rebar to reinforce or support us in creating consistency in our performance. This is another concept I learned from Carter Schelling.

In order to truly explain the power of structure and rebar, however, I need to first spend some time talking about the nature of behavioral change. Forgive me for going into this in some depth, but if you allow me to build this story from the ground up, I promise it will make perfect sense and you'll be able to fully appreciate the significance this Fundamental can play in your personal life as well as in your organization.

The Failure of Change Initiatives

Consider this: Every year, company executives spend huge amounts of time and money learning new ideas that will "take their organizations to another level." They hire consultants, develop catchy slogans, and then roll out the latest initiatives, strategic shifts, and innovative programs. Six months later, most of these programs are no longer operational, and the employees have learned to simply "wait it out" till the next great initiative comes down from corporate.

In much the same way, individuals spend literally billions of dollars in self-help books, tapes, seminars, and programs to learn the latest "secrets" to losing weight, getting fit, making money, and any host of other personal improvements, yet so few people ever successfully create lasting change in their lives. We learn new skills easily, agree that they make great sense, swear we'll do them for the rest of our lives, yet six months later no one is still practicing the recently acquired skills.

Why is this? Because few people ever learn the keys to lasting change: structure and accountability.

The Role of Inertia

Remember, as a schoolchild, learning about inertia in science class? Well, inertia acts on our own lives in a very similar manner to the way it operates in physics. Absent some new force, objects (or people) will tend to continue along the same path they're currently on. A habit is a human example of inertia. If I'm in the habit of eating junk food, I will continue that habit unless some new force is applied to disrupt the habit. If I'm in the habit of making sales presentations in a certain manner, I'll continue that routine as well, unless again some new force disrupts the habit.

Habits (and inertia) can be both good and bad. Being in the habit of brushing my teeth each morning and evening is a useful habit. The habit serves to continue the status quo—regardless of whether that status quo is good or bad, healthy or unhealthy. The key to success, then, is the letting go of bad habits and the adoption of new and healthier ones. But if habits, by definition, are ingrained, repetitive, inertia-like behaviors, how do we change them? The understanding of how new habits replace old ones is the most important element in creating lasting change.

Creating Change: Short-term vs. Long-term

What it takes to create short-term change is distinctly different from what it takes to create long-term change. Short-term change, as we will see, can be accomplished through the application of intense force, e.g., passion, motivation, desire, excitement. This energy creates the force necessary to disrupt our current patterns or habits. The deeper the current habit being disrupted, the greater the force necessary to affect it. The less ingrained the current habit, the less force that is required for disruption.

The problem is that it's quite difficult, if not impossible, to sustain this force. This is because the force requires energy—physical, emotional, and psychological. Since we have a finite amount of energy to expend (of course the amount varies for each person, yet is still finite for that person) in a day, the continued application of energy to change a deeply ingrained habit ultimately saps us.

In the early days of embarking on the new program, we're filled with passion and excitement for our goal. We can picture the new, slimmer version of ourselves. We're determined to be the top salesperson in the company. This passion supplies the additional energy necessary to disrupt the current habits. However, as this passion predictably wanes, so does the energy, and without this extra energy, we sink back into our old, deeply ingrained habits, and the new program falls by the wayside.

So how do we convert this early passion into long-lasting change? To understand this, we need to understand the different requirements of long-term change.

Long-term Change

Remember when you first learned to drive? There was so much to keep in mind—checking the speedometer, checking the rear view mirror, timing the clutch with proper gear shifting, properly positioning yourself within the lane, etc. Thinking of all these things and remembering them took tremendous energy. Today, no doubt most of these functions are practically automatic. They no longer require any thought (or energy) at all. The actions virtually happen without you even being conscious of them. Once these steps became ingrained habits, they ceased to require you to invest energy, thereby freeing that energy to be used elsewhere. In fact, you can perform all of the necessary functions of driving while at the same time carrying on a conversation or listening to an audio book.

So the process of adopting new habits, then, is one of heavy initial energy investment (to disrupt the inertia), then ultimately reduced energy investment as inertia acts to keep the new behavior in place and form a habit. The key step in this process is the conversion of the new behavior (as the energy wanes) into habit. This is the critical point where most people fail. If we don't successfully make this conversion, we sink back into old habits. If we do make the conversion, a new habit replaces the old one.

The Role of Rebar

The key to the conversion is structure or "rebar." Remember my construction analogy? Just as rebar adds extra strength to concrete, behavioral structure serves as a crutch to support us in that critical phase between the ebbing of our passion and the ingraining of our new habit. Again, in the beginning, our own excitement and passion are enough to get the new behavior started. In the end, inertia will keep it going. But how do we get from Stage 1 to Stage 3 without sinking back into old habits? That's where we need the "crutch" or extra support that properly designed structure and accountability can provide.

When I use the term "structure" in the context of behavioral change, I'm referring to the systems and processes we can create to help support us in more regularly doing the behavior we want. There are many useful forms of structure, limited only by your own creativity. Let me give you some examples.

Examples of Structure

Charts are one of the simplest and most effective types of structure. For years I knew that, as a runner, I needed to be more consistent in my stretching if I was to stay healthy, but I hate stretching. I find it boring and uncomfortable. So I created charts that I posted in my basement where I recorded the number of minutes of stretching I did each day. I also posted a goal for total annual stretching and graphed my performance vs. goal on a monthly basis. This simple system helped me to be far more consistent (I was not going to enter a zero on the chart!) and to stretch for longer periods of time than I would have on my own. Most importantly, it kept me engaged long enough (when the initial motivation waned) for a habit to be created.

Checklists are another amazingly simple example of structure. One of the observations we had at RSI was that if we brought in a new account in a complete and thorough fashion from the very beginning, the chances for long-term success rose dramatically. Yet there are many pieces to doing this well, and there are many different people who are involved. The chances that everyone always does their part right are slim indeed. So we identified the desired process, assigned tasks to the appropriate people, and then set up a checklist for all tasks with a place for sign-offs by the responsible person upon completion. What a simple way to help ensure that all steps are taken every time. Notice how "unsophisticated" this is, and yet how dramatically it improves the probability of success. Good structure is most often simple and unsophisticated.

Measurements are classic examples of structure or "rebar," as long as they are posted. If we want to improve the speed with which we answer the phones, nothing works better than measuring it and posting the results. This causes us to change our behavior in order to achieve the best posted numbers. As we continue the changed behavior (in response to the numbers) long enough, this now becomes a habit, and it no longer is as difficult to sustain.

In my experience, one of the most effective types of rebar is "routine." By this, I mean doing something at the same time every day or every week. For example, when it comes to exercise, you will be far more likely to succeed if you exercise every day first thing in the morning, or every day after work, rather than whenever you get the chance. The reason is simple and goes back to the issue of energy. When we exercise at the same time every day, it becomes part of our unthinking routine and becomes automatic. It no longer requires much mental energy to decide to do it because it's simply part of a normal day. When we fit it in wherever we can, we constantly have to make choices about whether to exercise at this moment or whether to do something else. This requires extra energy that becomes difficult to sustain.

Helping salespeople make cold calls is another good example of the power of routine. Since cold calling is the least enjoyable part of any salesperson's job, most tend to find ingenious ways to avoid it. They plan on making their calls when they "have a chance," which never seems to happen as frequently as necessary. However, by creating a routine, we can overcome this challenge. For example, if the salesperson makes calls every Monday and Wednesday mornings from 8:30 to 11:30, schedules all appointments for Tuesdays and Thursdays, and does paperwork Fridays, we remove the "willpower battle." We no longer have to fight with ourselves and exert so much energy to overcome our reluctance. We simply get in a habit.

To help me review our numbers, I used to ask for certain reports from each of my managers each month. It's far easier to establish that these reports are due on the same day each month rather than "sometime early in the month." If it's the same day, a routine can be established, and it can transition from a mental effort into a habit.

One of the most powerful forms of structure is accountability. Specifically, I mean proactively establishing accountability to another person for our actions. When I was in high school, I used to meet a friend of mine to run each morning before school at 6:00. Neither of us wanted to be the one to "miss an appointment," so we were always there. On dark, cold mornings, it's far easier to get out of bed if someone is waiting for you than if no one is. Arranging to meet someone every day at the gym at a specific time is far more likely to help you establish a habit than simply trying to demonstrate enough willpower on your own. Willpower takes tremendous emotional and psychological energy. Again, for 4-6 weeks when a new goal is exciting, pure excitement can generate the force necessary to break inertia. However, when this wears off, having to meet someone may be the difference that supports you in the transition to habit.

A Simple Example

Now that we understand the key elements to behavioral change, let's look at a simple example: Let's say two people each want to begin to keep a clean desk area (see Fundamental #25). Person A creates several systems for where to put the papers, folders, and other material that are usually left on her desk. She then arranges with her manager to do a weekly check-in on how her clean desk effort is going, and even sets a goal for the number of consecutive days with a clean desk and establishes a reward for herself for achieving her goal. She posts the number of "successful days in a row" in a prominent place outside her work area. Person B simply is determined to try his best to keep his desk clean. Which person is more likely to be successful in meeting their goal?

Let me give you one more example of something we did at RSI. We knew that giving our clients plenty of lead time to make health insurance renewal decisions helped them to feel more in control of their costs, and a key to giving them more time is to start the process earlier. Rather than simply saying "let's all work hard to start our renewals earlier," we put in place a series of structures and processes to help us achieve our goal. We built specific timelines identifying each step, when it needed to be completed, and by whom. We actually identified nearly 60 of these steps and assigned accountability and dates to each. We then used the process management tool we had built into our software system to automatically send reminders and track progress. Then we added measurement and began posting our results with regard to on-time completion of key process steps. These are all examples of structure and rebar that helped us to achieve higher performance.

Remember that structure and rebar can be as simple as a checklist or a chart, or as complex as a detailed reporting or measurement system. The important thing is to create a support mechanism that works for you.

A Bias for Structure and Rebar

Having a "bias" for structure and rebar means learning to put support in place for every new behavior. As soon as you identify a new goal, ask yourself what rebar you can create to assist you in developing a new habit to replace the old one. This is the critical element in creating long-lasting change. At RSI, whenever we were suggesting some new behavior, we learned to ask ourselves, "What rebar will we put in place to help us sustain this change?"

FUNDAMENTAL #29

The quality of your answers is directly related to the quality of your questions.

Learn to ask yourself, "What information is missing, that if I knew this, the best course of action would become self-evident."

Under the glass that covered my desk, I used to have a piece of paper that was positioned to face visitors to my office. On this paper I had typed the following four questions:

1. What's the situation?
2. What have you done so far?
3. What do you think you should do?
4. What are you asking of me?

It was fascinating to see how these questions could help to bring more clarity and focus to a conversation.

The first question, of course, asks for a brief synopsis of the overall situation. This is the who, what, where, when, and why of the current circumstances. If we don't understand the entire scenario, we may be too quick jump to incorrect conclusions (see Fundamental #30). Often, I would find that people would ask for my input on a situation without explaining enough of the story. This question serves to put the current dilemma into a broader context.

The second question asks for a progress report. It was usually the case that by the time someone came to me for assistance, they had already made several attempts to solve the problem on their own. In fact, this was normally the reason they were now coming to me. These attempts likely revealed important information not only about the situation, but also about how the person was approaching the problem. If I understood their approach, I could potentially use it as a teaching opportunity, for learning how to think about an issue is 90% of the solution.

The third question asks for the person's engagement. If we allow people to come to us and simply ask "What should I do," we're promoting intellectual laziness. Just giving them the answer creates dependency and doesn't serve their best interests or your own. When we ask another what they think they should do, it forces them to put the pieces together and form a game plan. And just as I noted in the second question, it gives you a window into understanding how they're processing the information. Helping them learn how to approach an issue is far more important in the long run than simply solving the current problem.

I always tried to use every situation as an opportunity to teach people how to think. I don't mean that in a derogatory way at all. Rather, I mean that if I could help people to learn good skills for evaluating an issue, then they would be able to use those skills to successfully navigate their way through any future problem they may encounter. This, in turn, creates an amazingly competent, flexible, and adaptable organization.

The fourth question on my list asks for clarity about my role in the exchange. I added this question as a result of many experiences where I found myself confused as to just what the person was looking for. Sometimes I found that after hearing the whole story, I realized that the problem was already solved and they just wanted to tell me about it. Other times, they were pretty sure what they should do but just wanted to bounce it off me first. Sometimes they were looking for permission to take an action, and still other times they had absolutely no clue what to do and needed direction. If I knew what role I was to play, it made it easier for me to listen with the appropriate intention.

After many years of working with people using these four questions, I began to notice something. I found that when people came to me for help and we began to go through the four questions, they were often working with an incomplete picture. In other words, they were trying to decide on a course of action ignorant of vital information. In fact, many times the reason they felt confused, and sometimes even paralyzed, in their decision-making was that they only had half the picture. It was then that I added the fifth question.

The Fifth Question

Here's the fifth key question:

5. What information is missing, that if you knew this, the best course of action would become self-evident?

This question asks the person to see the situation like a jigsaw puzzle and to identify the missing pieces. When we just start a jigsaw puzzle, each individual piece looks so disconnected from the whole that it's difficult (without looking at the box!) to see what the whole image will look like when completed. However, the more pieces we put in, the clearer the picture becomes, until we can eventually easily recognize the whole scene. Notice, also, that you don't need to have put in every single piece in order to get a good sense of the picture. I think decision-making is a lot like this.

At first, we're confused about what to do because we can't make sense of all the parts. The more we assemble the facts, though, the better our understanding becomes of our various options and, more often than not, the right course of action becomes truly obvious. While this sounds remarkably simple, it's fascinating to notice how often we try to make decisions based on particularly limited or incomplete information.

Admittedly, there are times we cannot gather *every* relevant fact or simply are faced with time constraints that don't allow the collection of all the facts. In fact, I once heard someone say that the higher you rise in an organization, the bigger the decisions you have to make, and the less information you have to make them!

We'll never have *all* the information, and we never have unlimited time to gather data. This is why it's so important to ask yourself this fifth question. If you look closely, the question doesn't ask for all information. Rather, it asks for those pieces of information that would make the right course of action obvious. Let me give you a rather mundane example to illustrate what I mean.

This past fall, my daughter began her freshman year of college. Like most young people today, she stays very connected to her world, primarily through her iPhone. As she moved into her dorm on her first day, she quickly discovered that AT&T coverage was abysmal in her dorm and, in fact, much of campus. She called me, terribly upset about this problem and wanting to know what she should do.

Let's set aside for the moment any editorial comments about how small an issue this really is and how we remember the days when we had to use hallway phones in the dorm when we were in college; the problem that my daughter faced was a typical one. She was frustrated and didn't know what to do. The reason she was so confused is that she had large gaps in her information that prevented her from seeing her options clearly, and thereby making it difficult to choose a smart course of action.

So, what information would she need to know for the best path to become clear? Let's make a list:

- Is there likely to be any change in AT&T's coverage on campus any time in the near future? If so, when?

- Do people have good coverage with Verizon or other carriers on campus?

- What would the cost be to terminate the AT&T coverage early?

- What would the cost be to buy a new phone with a different carrier?

- Can the current iPhone be switched over to Verizon? If so, at what cost? If not, what would a new iPhone with Verizon cost?

- Many upperclassmen on campus must have iPhones. How are they dealing with this issue? Perhaps they've found it to be not as significant a problem as it now seems.

All of these answers are relatively easy to discover with a pretty small investment of time. Armed with these answers, she could easily make a list of options, determine the advantages and disadvantages of each, and assess which option would make the most sense for her. The key step is simply identifying the missing pieces and then filling them in. Remember, we're not talking about every missing piece—just those that would make the picture clear. Without this, we're trying to make decisions in the dark. By the way, she ended up staying with AT&T and finding that it's annoying, but livable.

The key to asking quality questions is starting with the end in mind. In other words, if you're thoughtful about the information you're looking for, you can construct more specific, targeted questions to elicit that information. Often, poor questions are the result of not putting enough thought into what we're looking for. It's like stopping to ask someone for directions when we're not sure where we want to go. Know your destination and you'll be more effective in how you ask for directions.

The Art of Decision Making

Recently, I had a conversation with a college professor I know who teaches a business leadership development course. As she considered possible enhancements to the course's design, she was curious to know what I thought students should learn that would be most helpful in their leadership careers. Here's what I told her:

I said that if I had to choose one leadership skill over all others, it would be the ability to make good decisions. No matter what field we're in or what our specific responsibilities might be, we all have decisions to make every day. In fact, the same could certainly be said for all of us, whether we're in leadership roles or not. Our lives are filled with decisions, some large and others small. In large measure, our ability to make good decisions, defined as ones that have a higher probability of generating the outcome we want, determines our success. And good decision-making has, at its core, the ability to ask useful questions.

Incidentally, many people regard a decision as "good" when it yields a positive result. For example, if they were trying to choose between two stocks in which to invest and they choose Stock A, they would call it a good decision if it performed better than Stock B. I would disagree with this assessment.

For me, a good decision is about process, not outcome. If we asked the appropriate questions about both stocks, gathered the relevant information, and then made an intelligent choice based on which one had the highest probability of meeting our objectives, then it was a good decision. The rest is out of our control. Sometimes things happen that make a good decision yield a bad result. If several key executives in Company B were unexpectedly killed in a tragic accident and the stock dropped, it wouldn't mean you had made a bad decision. And conversely, if you choose which stock to invest in by flipping a coin and the one you chose doubled in value over the next year, I would not describe it as a good decision. I'd call it good "luck." Decision-making is not about luck. It's about making intelligent choices based on a thoughtful, analytic process.

The Five Components of Good Decisions

I think of the decision-making process as being composed of five simple steps:

1. **Defining the goal clearly**. It's surprising how often there is disagreement about the goal, particularly when multiple people are involved. Since the best decision is the one that has the greatest probability of achieving the goal, it's essential that we have absolute clarity about how we define the goal.

2. **Gathering the relevant data**. This is the fifth of my key questions. Learn to identify what's missing that, when supplied, will make the picture clear. Then gather that data.

3. **Determining the set of options**. Once we have a clear picture based on having all the relevant facts, we can develop a list of possible actions we could take. There are almost always multiple ways of solving a given problem.

4. **Identifying the advantages and disadvantages of each option**. Undoubtedly, each option has positives and negatives associated with it. Listing these for each option helps us to see more clearly the potential risks and rewards of our choices.

5. **Selecting the option that has the highest likelihood of achieving the desired outcome**. Good decision-making is a game of probability. We can't guarantee the outcome. We can only make the choice that has the best probability, based on our analysis, of yielding the outcome we're looking for.

If we're skilled decision-makers, we're able to face almost any situation and figure out what to do. It's hard to think of a more valuable leadership ability than that. And the cornerstone of it all is the practice of asking quality questions; for the quality of your answers is directly related to the quality of your questions.

FUNDAMENTAL #30

Be quick to ask and slow to judge.

Learn to gather the facts before making judgments. Be curious about additional information that may yield a more complete picture.

How many times have we seen a situation where we had bits of information, completed the rest of the picture in our own mind, and then came to a conclusion that ultimately proved to be incorrect? I find this to be particularly common when it comes to making interpretations about other people and their motivations. Let's examine this more closely with a simple, even mundane example.

We had a rule at RSI that it was the responsibility of each person to clean their own dishes as well as those used with a visiting client. Imagine that one day, you walk past the kitchen and see a manager place several dishes in the sink and then leave. Angry at the blatant disregard of our common understanding and courtesy, you grumble to a co-worker about how the rules don't seem to apply to managers. Further, you carry this view of the world with you into other interactions and interpret what you see from this perspective.

But might there be more to the picture? Try this, for example. When you explored further, you learned that a co-worker had been in a client meeting and was carrying a load of dishes back to the kitchen and was also trying to juggle several proposal binders. Seeing this, the manager quickly offered to carry the dishes back to the kitchen. At the moment you witnessed the event in the kitchen, the co-worker was still engaged in a conversation with the client and had not yet gotten back to the kitchen to take care of the dirty dishes. Had you known the rest of the story, you would have been pleased that you work in a place where people are quick to assist each other and you would carry this different view with you into other interactions.

The Impact of Our Filters

Remember in Fundamental #9, I talked about the impact that our "filters" have on how we perceive or interpret our observations? Think about these two filters and how they affect what we "see." In the first instance, we left the kitchen grousing about the double standard that exists at our office. In the second instance, however, we left the kitchen thankful for the sense of camaraderie and support that we have. These represent two entirely different lenses through which to see everything else that happens following that moment. Can you see the significant impact this has?

Let me ask you this. Was the first interpretation a reasonable conclusion to draw from the facts that you observed? You witnessed the manager carry the dishes to the kitchen, drop them in the sink, and walk away. Here's one of the most interesting conundrums about these scenarios and others like them: Most of the time, the conclusions we draw represent a perfectly reasonable way of adding up the facts. It's just that while it may be reasonable, it also may be flat-out wrong! And the impact of it being wrong can often be quite significant.

One of the keys here is understanding the difference between a "fact" and an "interpretation." It's a *fact* that the manager left the dishes in the sink. "The manager doesn't care about the rules" is just one *interpretation* from that fact; but as we've seen, there are other available interpretations from that fact. This distinction is critical to understand in order to appreciate the power inherent in this Fundamental, so let's take a closer look.

Events vs. Interpretations

Every day, all around us, people do an infinite number of things. They smile. They frown. They go to meetings. They make comments. They play games. They make phone calls. They exercise. They read a book. And on and on. Let's call these occurrences "events."

When we observe these events, we interpret what we see and attach a meaning to it. For example, we see someone eating dinner alone in a restaurant, and we draw conclusions about what's going on. We create a story in our mind that explains what we see. The person must be single. Or the person must be lonely. Let's call these stories "interpretations."

Note that we create stories or interpretations for things we hear as well as things we see. We hear that someone wasn't invited to the wedding and we create a story that they had a falling out with the bride. We hear that someone was fired and we create an interpretation that their boss was unfair.

The problem is that we often link the event and the interpretation so closely, that we effectively collapse them into one. We treat our story as if it were a fact. Let me give you an example.

I'll hear someone say, "Mary doesn't respect me." When I ask more about this, I'll hear all about how Mary was late for an appointment with the speaker for the third time in a row. The "event" is Mary being late. The "interpretation" is that Mary doesn't respect me.

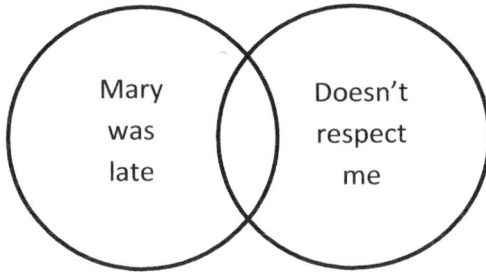

The two overlapping circles represent our tendency to fold these ideas into one; but they *are* two entirely separate notions. One is an observable fact. Mary was definitely late. The other is simply the conclusion we drew from this observable fact.

Why is this distinction so critical? Because opening up some "space" between the event and its interpretation gives us a whole new range of possibilities, and with it, a whole new range of potential responses.

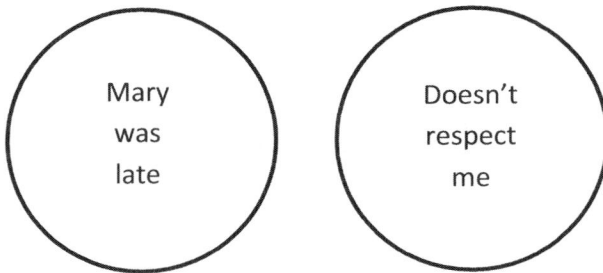

If we allow the two to be collapsed into one, however, then our only possible conclusion is that Mary doesn't respect me. And if this is true, there are a limited number of ways I could deal with Mary and her lack of respect.

If I see "Mary doesn't respect me" as an interpretation, then I can be open to the possibility that there may be other reasonable interpretations from this same event. Maybe Mary thought the meeting was a different time. Maybe she was stuck in traffic. Maybe she was in a client meeting that was running longer than planned. Maybe she didn't know there had been a meeting called. Maybe her child was sick. Maybe her car broke down. There may be a whole host of other scenarios. The important point is that we don't know how to interpret it. All that we *do* know is that Mary was late.

When we realize that there could, in fact, be many different explanations for an event, we turn on our curiosity and we ask more questions. This curiosity gives us a greater range of options for how to respond. It puts us in a position of much greater personal power because we have choices.

When I took over managing my team, there were a few people who seemed frustrated about their work, customers, and the company in general. My initial reaction to their words was that I had a couple of bad apples here and that I might eventually need to make some personnel changes. I was getting trapped in a "filter" of mine that had me too focused on how their frustrations were being voiced as opposed to being curious and finding out more of the story.

As time went on, I was able to get closer to the team's day-to-day work, establish greater trust, and gather further details that helped me see the root cause of some of their frustrations. Ironically, as my "filter" changed and I realized the value I could derive from being quick to ask and slow to judge, it seemed like the words they were using to express frustration become more forwarding and less complaining in nature. What a difference perspective makes!
-Bob F.

The Value of Curiosity

I'm always surprised at how quick many people are to jump to conclusions in their interpretation of events—especially when the event seems to run counter to what our experience might normally suggest. For example, let's suppose you know from your experience that your manager, Jane, is always fair in her performance evaluations, and that she works closely with her team to help each member succeed. Yesterday, you heard from a co-worker that Jim, a member of Jane's team, was let go without any warning at all. Your co-worker is incensed at how unfair this is, and is grumbling around the office to anyone who'll listen. It's startling to watch how many people join in the anger and frustration without stopping to question if there might be more to the story.

When coaching people through these situations, I always remind people to simply slow down, to not be in such a rush to judgment. Sometimes we just need to take a breath and create that "space" I men-

One Sunday, my son moved my car in order to vacuum it. I was gone for the day at a soccer tournament, and when I spoke to my son on the phone later in the day, he told me there was a problem with the car. Certain that whatever the problem was had to be his fault, I had to remind myself to suspend my judgment and wait till I return home to get the facts.

When I got home, we went outside together to talk about what happened. He told me that while backing the car out of the garage he heard a loud pop. At this point I wanted to blame him but Fundamental #6 came to mind. As I asked a few more questions and had the car checked out, I discovered that I had a cracked manifold—something that was certainly not caused by my son. By being quicker to ask questions and slower to judge, I saved an argument and found out what the real problem was.

-Doug B.

tioned between the event and our interpretation.

Once we've created that space, we need to become curious. If I've always known Jane to be a fair person who really is "for" her teammates (see Fundamental #20), then it would seem awfully surprising and inconsistent for her to have simply let Jim go without any warning. I wonder what else might have been taking place? Maybe there's a larger picture or there's more information that would have me see this situation quite differently. If appropriate (in this case, some answers might be confidential), what questions might I ask (see Fundamental #29), and of whom, that might give me a more complete picture?

First Impressions

In addition to our tendency to judge situations based on an incomplete picture, think about how quickly we typically judge people. What criteria do we use? For most of us, we quickly assess others based on what they're wearing, their demeanor, their posture, whether they have piercings or visible tattoos, and a host of other readily observable characteristics. Have you ever considered the impact of these judgments? A particular experience I've had several times always serves as a reminder to me to try harder to resist my natural inclination to judge too swiftly.

In the past 16 years, I've participated in eight Outward Bound wilderness expeditions. These have been amazing trips full of challenge, learning, beauty, and introspection. A typical Outward Bound expedition is composed of a crew of 8-12 people plus two instructors. Participants come from all walks of life and all backgrounds, with the only common denominator being that we all signed up for the same course.

Our adventure always begins at an airport in the vicinity of our destination. Here, we meet the people who will be on our trip, load our gear into a van, and begin traveling to a trailhead somewhere in the wilderness. The van ride is usually spent exchanging personal stories as we get to know each other.

Here's what I notice on every trip: As soon as I see the people I'll be with, I immediately begin to form judgments. "I like this person." "She seems nice." "That person over there looks really annoying." "I hope I'm not stuck with this person." "I can't believe I'm going to have to spend the next eight days with that guy." All of these assessments are formed with little to no real information about the person—just my first impressions.

But here's where it gets interesting. Because I'm literally stuck with these people for the next 8-10 days, 24 hours a day, I have no choice but to get to know them. And virtually without exception, I come to see that they're all wonderful people with a lot to offer. They each have their own personal stories of challenges faced, of triumphs and of disappointments— and there are lessons I can learn from every one of them. Certainly, some I enjoy more than others, but I gain a deeper appreciation for the fullness and depth of each person in a way that I wouldn't have if I weren't stuck with them.

This experience always causes me to think about all the people that I shut out of my life based on a quick assessment. How many people have I not gotten to know because I too swiftly determined that I don't like them? What learning have I missed out on? Who and what might you be inadvertently eliminating from your own life because of your tendency to make snap judgments? I always come back from an Outward Bound trip determined to be more curious and slower to judge, though I admit I often fall short of my goal.

When we learn to suspend our judgment and become more curious, we gain more choice and flexibility. We have more options for how to respond. We open ourselves to new possibilities. Learn to resist the temptation to "jump to conclusions" before you have more information. Be curious to learn as much as you can to gain a greater understanding of the entire situation. As we gather additional information, remember Fundamental #9 – Work from the assumption that people are good, fair, and honest, and Fundamental #18 – Listen generously. Make your starting point the most generous view you can have.

There is great power in gaining a deeper appreciation and understanding of each other. Deeper understanding begins with genuine curiosity. Genuine curiosity begins when we are quick to ask and slow to judge.

> *I'll never forget one of the most important conversations I ever had—and I almost "chickened out!" My supervisor was reducing her work hours and we had agreed that I would take over some of her responsibilities in exchange for additional compensation. Before this became "official" however, the President said he wanted to explore other options. I was devastated and hurt, convinced that he disliked me and didn't think I was competent.*
>
> *I realized I needed to talk to him directly. Though it was hard, I reminded myself to let go of my predetermined conclusions and be more curious to learn the rest of the story. To my surprise, I learned that he did respect me and that he just wanted to consider all options in order to make the best overall decision. I really felt listened to and saw a much different picture. Though I did eventually get the position, the more important thing I learned was the value of being quicker to ask and slower to judge. I try to remind myself of this every day.*
> *-Maureen W.*

CONCLUSION

Just prior to retiring, I went to lunch with my entire management team. I was completing 27 years of work at RSI, and the managers were looking for any last-minute pearls of wisdom. As the dishes were cleared, someone asked me what I was most proud of in my career, and what advice I would offer to them as they sought to carry on what we had started together. This is what I told them.

I said that there were three things that stood out for me more than anything else, and these were the things I'd urge them to continue:

1. **Our commitment to A+ness**. I was proud of how much our people cared about doing their best work. And not just some of our people. *All* of our people. Without exception. They may have varied over the years in terms of their skills and abilities, but they never varied in their passion for excellence. Creating an environment that cultivated and nourished this passion was in no small part responsible for much of our success.

2. **Our commitment to values-based behavior**. The creation of the Fundamentals and the many ways we made them part of our everyday life is, of course, the substance of this book. But no book can adequately describe the enthusiasm our people showed for living their lives according to a code. I believe that most people thirst for such an environment, where values are real and

they're practiced on a daily basis. Unfortunately, most people have been so disillusioned by the failure of their organizations and their leaders to stand on firm ground when it comes to values, that they've almost given up. I'm proud of our steadfast, unrelenting commitment to behaving in a way that's consistent with the values we hold dear.

3. **Our commitment to keeping things fun**. Little in life is worth doing if we can't laugh and smile and have fun along the way. I'm proud that we never took ourselves too seriously. That we never forgot that uncontrollable fits of laughter are good. That giggles can be contagious. That it's important to enjoy each day and the people we spend it with. And that fart machines are, indeed, funny.

If I have a hope for this book, it's that you've enjoyed reading it, and that in doing so, you've found inspiration and insight. Inspiration to lead both your organization and your life in a way that embodies the values about which you're most passionate; and insight into how you can effectively accomplish doing just that.

Warmly,

David

AFTERWORD

If I perhaps left you wondering why I retired, and what eventually happened to RSI, let me briefly share with you the next chapter in that story.

Not surprisingly, given our success and the reputation we had built, we became an attractive target for larger consulting and brokerage firms looking to grow through acquisition. At the same time, we recognized the strategic value of having access to the greater resources that were becoming necessary to compete in an increasingly challenging economic environment. And so, in May of 2008, we agreed to sell RSI to Arthur J. Gallagher & Co. (AJG), a multi-billion-dollar, publicly-traded company, and one of the largest insurance brokerages in the world.

As you would imagine, selecting a partner who would be a strong cultural fit was a major factor in our choice of AJG. Run by Pat Gallagher, the grandson of the founder, AJG's operating values were remarkably similar to our own.

I stayed on for two years, continuing to lead RSI as a division of Gallagher Benefit Services (GBS), its subsidiary focused exclusively on the employee benefits portion of the insurance industry. During this transition time, we continued to use the Fundamentals as the basis for our organizational culture, though we recognized that it would eventually become appropriate to take on the language of Gallagher's "shared values." These values were originally written by Arthur J. Gallagher's son, Bob (Pat's uncle), and are known as the Gallagher Way.

Having accomplished everything that I had wanted to in the insurance industry, in 2010 I decided it was time for me to explore new ways to use all that I had learned. This book, in fact, is just the beginning of that process. I was confident that the leadership team I had groomed was ready to carry on successfully in my absence, and they've done just that.

As for the Fundamentals, they continued to be practiced formally through the end of 2010, after which the shift was made to begin using the Gallagher Way. The weekly rituals (weekly e-mails, first agenda item in meetings, etc.) remain, and are now based on the language of Gallagher's shared values rather than the language of the Fundamentals. Of course, as I'm told by so many of my former staff, the Fundamentals continue to live on as strongly as ever in the way people conduct themselves, both at work and in their personal lives as well.

Appendix A

The Original Fundamentals Card

Appendix B

Initial e-mail introducing the Fundamentals

From: David Friedman
Sent: Sunday, February 22, 2004 10:46 AM
To: All Employees
Subject: RSI Fundamental #1

By now, you've each received a copy of what I call the RSI Fundamentals. I'd like you to study these and to keep this card with you at all times. You'll notice that I've grouped the Fundamentals into four categories: Core Values, Focus on Service, The Collaborative Way, and Personal Effectiveness. These fundamentals serve as a practical guide for our behavior; for as people, and as an organization, we *are* how we *behave*. We are not what is written on our walls and posted around the office. We are not what we talk about or even what we believe in. No, the real evidence of who we are is in the behaviors that show up on a daily basis – the behaviors that our clients, carriers, co-workers, friends, and family actually observe. We are how we behave.

Each week, we'll be featuring one of our "Fundamentals." I'll begin the week by sharing with you the text of the Fundamental as well as some thoughts and further explanation. I'll do this through both e-mail and voicemail. Additionally, I'm asking the managers to feature the week's Fundamental in departmental meetings, one-on-one meetings, and in various conversations throughout the week. I'm also asking each of you to give your own extra focus to the featured Fundamental over the course of the week. Think about what it means to you. Think about how you can demonstrate this principle even more strongly than you have in the past. Think about new ways to apply the idea in your everyday work.

Organizational (and personal) success comes from having the will and the discipline to do the basics right, day after day, week after week. Focusing on our Fundamentals is an important part of this effort, and an important part of what separates RSI from the rest.

David

Appendix C

In preparation for passing the baton to the management team, these were my thoughts and observations on the Fundamentals after the completion of the first 30 weeks.

From: David Friedman
Sent: Saturday, September 11, 2004 5:23 AM
To: All Employees
Subject: Thoughts and observations on the Fundamentals

As we complete the first 30 weeks of our focus on the Fundamentals, I want to let you know what's coming next, and just as importantly, I want to share some thoughts and observations with you.

As to what's next, we'll begin again by starting with Fundamental #1 and cycling through all 30 over a 30-week period. However, this time around members of our leadership team (Larry, Sharyn, Bill, Ralph, Bonnie, and Kurt) will be responsible for sending out the weekly voicemail and e-mail, adding their own thoughts on the application of the week's Fundamental. We'll also begin to institutionalize the practice of beginning any meeting at RSI with a 3-4 minute discussion of the Fundamental of the Week. This discussion can be led by any participant in the meeting, and I would encourage you to step forward and volunteer as a way of deepening your own understanding and practice of the Fundamentals.

Candidly, some might look at what we do at RSI as pretty strange! So why do we continue to focus so much effort on the Fundamentals? The answer can be found in three important concepts:

1. Cultural Alignment

2. Cultural Integrity

3. Cultural Consistency

Put simply, "cultural alignment" is when all members of the organization share common beliefs about core values and principles. I've long maintained that cultural alignment is a huge business differentiator because it leads to increased organizational speed and effectiveness. Like the scull on a river with all oarsman rowing in perfect synchronicity, an organization where all participants are working in concert has less "drag," moves more speedily, and meets challenges more effectively.

"Cultural integrity" occurs when our actions match our stated values. We may all share common beliefs and hold common points of view about guiding principles, but unless our actual behavior reflects these values, we won't all be on "the same page." Worse, a disconnect between values and behavior often leads to skepticism and cynicism, two forces that can quickly destroy the best and most well-intentioned efforts of any organization.

When our actions <u>always</u> match our stated values, we have "cultural consistency." People know what to expect of us simply by looking at our guiding principles. Decisions are made in the context of a philosophical framework. We ask ourselves, "What is our principle about this?" or "what do our values say we should do?"

The RSI Fundamentals are a blueprint for both our values and our behavior. By embracing them as a standard, we create cultural alignment. By putting them into everyday practice, we produce cultural integrity. By constantly teaching, deepening, and reinforcing them, we achieve cultural consistency.

While my experience tells me that this emphasis on culture is a critical element of organizational success, I must also confess that the reasons for our intense focus go deeper than that. I believe that values and principles matter in and of themselves, independent of the likely business result. I believe that working in an environment where predictable, commonly held principles guide action is inherently rewarding and, in some way, resonates inside our souls like a perfectly tuned instrument. It simply feels right on the most basic of levels, and as such, needs no business-case justification. Values and principles are like guideposts that light our way in a world that can often be confusing and difficult to navigate. Our practice of the Fundamentals is the cornerstone of this effort.

I want to thank you for helping RSI to stake out a leadership position in our industry as well as our community. We are not normal, and I'm thankful for that.

Warmly,

David

Appendix D

RSI Annual Fundamentals Survey

This is the text of the questions asked on the survey sent each year to all clients, vendors/suppliers, and employees. The instructions were to indicate the degree of frequency with which the respondent observed our behaviors to be consistent with each statement. The choices were:

Almost Always   Usually   Sometimes   Seldom   Never   Don't Know

1. *Core Values – These values have been a cornerstone of our success for more than 20 years.*

   Fundamental #1: Do what's best for the client.

   RSI staff act in a way that puts the best interests of the client first.

   Fundamental #2: Check the ego at the door.

   RSI staff demonstrate a willingness to set their egos aside and focus on solving the problem and/or doing what's right.

   Fundamental #3: Practice A+ness as a way of life.

   RSI staff demonstrate an intense focus on the quality of everything they touch.

Fundamental #4: Take the extra time to do things right the first time.

RSI staff take care to see that work is correct the first time it's done, thereby reducing or eliminating rework.

Fundamental #5: Seek to create win/win solutions.

RSI staff look for solutions that satisfy the interests of all concerned.

Fundamental #6: Practice blameless problem solving.

RSI staff refrain from placing blame, and instead, focus their attention on solving current problems and preventing future ones.

Fundamental #7: Make decisions that reflect a reverence for long-term relationships.

RSI staff act in a way that shows long-term thinking and value for relationships.

Fundamental #8: Maintain a solution orientation rather than a problem orientation.

RSI staff focus their thought, creativity, and energy on finding solutions, not dwelling on problems.

Fundamental #9: Work from the assumption that people are good, fair, and honest.

RSI staff approach others from a perspective of trust and assume positive intent.

Fundamental #10: Keep things fun.

RSI staff demonstrate a sense of light-heartedness, happiness, and optimism.

2. *Focus on Service — These habits help create extraordinary service experiences.*

Fundamental #11: Create a feeling of warmth and friendliness in every client interaction.

Interacting with RSI staff is a pleasant, warm, and friendly experience.

Fundamental #12: Practice the "Human Touch."

RSI staff do the little things to show that they truly care about people as individuals.

Fundamental #13: Communicate to be understood.

RSI staff speak and write in ways that make it easy to understand their message.

Fundamental #14: Set and ask for expectations.

RSI staff are careful to communicate about expectations so that everyone is working from the same set of assumptions.

Fundamental #15: Make voicemail a valuable tool.

RSI staff update their voicemail daily and use their voicemail greeting to set expectations and to create a feeling of friendliness.

Fundamental #16: Follow-up everything.

RSI staff regularly follow-up on open issues to be sure that tasks are completed as expected.

Fundamental #17: Be punctual.

RSI staff are on time for appointments, meetings, and phone calls, and demonstrate a respect for the time of others.

3. *The Collaborative Way – These practices enable us to work powerfully together as a team.*

Fundamental #18: Listen generously.

RSI staff are good listeners. They listen fully and without judgment.

Fundamental #19: Speak straight.

RSI staff speak honestly and directly, even when topics are difficult or awkward to discuss. They speak in a way that enables positive action.

Fundamental #20: Be for each other.

RSI staff demonstrate a commitment to the success of others, providing rigorous support of each other when necessary.

Fundamental #21: Honor commitments.

RSI staff do what they say they will do, when they say they will do it. If a commitment becomes impossible to keep, they notify others at the earliest possible time in order to discuss alternatives.

Fundamental #22: Be a source for acknowledgement and appreciation.

RSI staff express meaningful and appropriate recognition and appreciate up, down, and across organizations.

4. *Personal Effectiveness – These behaviors help us to achieve greater personal, and by extension, organizational success.*

Fundamental #23: Take responsibility.

RSI staff act powerfully and take responsibility for results, rather than being "bystanders" or "victims."

Fundamental #24: Appearance counts.

RSI staff present themselves neatly and professionally – in their dress, their materials, and in their environment.

Fundamental #25: Being organized makes a difference.

RSI staff demonstrate a sense of orderliness and an ability to effectively manage multiple tasks.

Fundamental #26: Double-check all work.

RSI staff double-check all work, catching errors before work is presented to end users.

Fundamental #27: Look ahead and anticipate.

RSI staff prepare for future events effectively by looking ahead and anticipating needs, challenges, and opportunities.

Fundamental #28: Have a bias for structure and rebar.

RSI staff look for ways to build systems and processes to ensure consistent performance.

Fundamental #29: The quality of your answers is directly related to the quality of your questions.

RSI staff ask thoughtful and insightful questions that help get to the heart of issues.

Fundamental #30: Be quick to ask and slow to judge.

RSI staff suspend their judgments until they have a complete picture. They're curious and ask probing questions to discover more information.

Appendix E

Here's a list of the books I referred to throughout my writing. They're listed here under the chapter, and in the order, in which I discussed them.

Institutionalizing Values

> Good to Great, Why Some Companies Make the Leap . . . and Others Don't, by Jim Collins (2001). Harper-Collins Publishers.

> Based on years of research, Collins identifies the key factors that determine which companies are able to go beyond just being "good," and reach ever higher levels of success.

Fundamental #1

> The Speed of Trust, The One Thing That Changes *Everything*, by Stephen M. R. Covey with Rebecca R. Merrill (2006). Free Press.

> This is truly one of my favorites. Covey presents a compelling case for how greater trust generates greater profits, and then goes on to examine the specific behaviors that lead to increasing trust.

> Getting Naked: A Business Fable About Shedding The Three Fears That Sabotage Client Loyalty, by Patrick Lencioni (2010). Jossey-Bass.

> This is an absolute must-read for anyone in a consulting role. Through a fictional story, Lencioni shows how making

ourselves more "vulnerable" or "naked" for our clients actually increases customer loyalty. One of the most useful business books I've ever read.

Fundamental #5

Smart Negotiating, How to Make Good Deals in the Real World, by James C. Freund (1992). Simon & Schuster.

While he provides plenty of specific tips that are useful for negotiating, the key to this book is Freund's underlying point of view that the only truly successful negotiations are ones that create win/win outcomes.

Fundamental #12

Swim with the Sharks Without Being Eaten Alive: Outsell, Outmanage, Outmotivate, and Outnegotiate Your Competition, by Harvey Mackay (1988). Fawcett Columbine.

This is the book that made Mackay famous. He shares lots of great ideas from his own personal experience as a CEO, told in a particularly down-to-earth style. The Mackay 66 is his customer profile tool that I reference.

Fundamental #23

Man's Search for Meaning, by Victor E. Frankl (2006). Beacon Press.

Frankl was an Austrian neurologist and psychiatrist who was imprisoned in the Nazi concentration camps in World War II. As both a survivor and a psychiatrist, his observations about our ability to choose our own attitudes and the role that our attitudes play is incredibly insightful. This is an inspiring book.

Unbroken: A World War II Story of Survival, Resilience, and Redemption, by Laura Hillenbrand (2010). Random House.

This is the amazing story of Louis Zamperini, an Olympic runner and aviator whose plane went down in the South Pacific during World War II. There are few stories of survival that can match this one. Like Frankl, Zamperini observes firsthand the difference attitude makes in our ability to survive the most grueling challenges one can imagine.

Your Erroneous Zones, by Dr. Wayne W. Dyer (2001). Avon Books.

More than anything else, this book is about taking control of our lives. In his crystal-clear style, Dyer shows us our emotional "blind spots" and helps us to see that we can take responsibility for how we live our lives. This is one of the best self-help books ever written.

Black Boy, by Richard Wright (1945). Harper & Bros.

I read this book in high school and have never forgotten the incredible story of how Wright overcame almost absurd obstacles to become an educated man and a best-selling author. Anyone who thinks it's impossible to rise above an underprivileged background needs to read this book. It's truly an inspiring story.

The Aladdin Factor, by Jack Canfield and Mark Victor Hansen (1995). Berkley Publishing Group.

This is a fascinating book by the same people who wrote the "Chicken Soup" series. Filled with lots of stories, the authors examine why we're often hesitant to simply ask for what we want, and the amazing impact that asking can have on our lives.

The E-Myth Revisited, Why Most Small Businesses Don't Work and What to Do About It, by Michael E. Gerber (2001). Harper-Collins Publishers.

This is a classic book about the difference between working *in* the business and working *on* the business. Gerber shows why small business leaders typically get so caught up in running the day-to-day operations that they fail to build the systems and processes that are necessary for longer-term success. He's very big on standardization and draws heavily from lessons learned in franchises.

ACKNOWLEDGEMENTS

There are a number of people I'd like to thank for their role in helping me learn the lessons I've been privileged to share with you in this book, and a number of others I want to thank for their role in the actual production of the book.

My father, Stan Friedman, invited me to join him in the insurance business, and was my first business teacher. From the beginning, he treated me as an equal and encouraged my development as a professional. Throughout his career, and our work together, he was a shining example of what would later become the first two Fundamentals—Do what's best for the client, and Check the ego at the door. None of this would have happened without him.

I met Carter Schelling, the Chairman of 3655, Inc., in 1995, as I was trying to make the transition from being an insurance salesperson to being a company president. More than any other person, Carter was responsible for helping me to learn the essential skills of business leadership. From the beginning of our relationship, he has challenged my thinking, and challenged me to be the best leader I could be. He remains an important part of my support team.

Carter also introduced me to Lloyd Fickett, the author of The Collaborative Way. Lloyd and The Collaborative Way have had a significant influence on how I think and how I communicate. I am not overstating the case when I say that practicing The Collaborative Way had a monumental impact on the organizational culture we created at RSI. Lloyd continues to be a trusted friend and supporter.

I had the good fortune to work alongside my brother, Larry Friedman, for 22 of my 27 years at RSI. He has been a vital sounding board for me, and a co-author of much of our organizational culture. Without his selflessness, his possibility-thinking, and his generous spirit, we would not have been able to achieve the many successes that we did.

Terry Delaney and Jeff Ohlstein were two of the original "partners" of RSI. Their complete trust in me was instrumental in helping me to successfully take on the leadership mantel. Knowing I always had their unquestioned support gave me the intellectual freedom to follow often unconventional paths in pursuit of A+ness.

Early in my leadership career, I learned the importance of having a skilled and cohesive management team. There is simply no way we could have accomplished what we did, nor could I have grown as I did, without the support of my team. Each of them developed into skilled and savvy managers, and they became great friends of mine as well. I honestly cannot imagine a better team than my brother Larry, Bill Kaiser, Bonnie Antonelli, Ralph Catillo, Kurt Hettel, Sharyn Spitznagel, Christine Ament, and Bob Flanders.

Finally, with respect to my learning, I would be remiss if I didn't make note of the significant role that our entire RSI staff played. In so many ways, RSI was different than any other company. It was a community of people committed to each other, to our clients, and to the relentless pursuit of A+ness. Their willingness to buy into the culture we were co-creating made it a truly special environment; and that environment became the classroom in which I learned the lessons in this book. I am indebted to them for their unwavering support of me as their leader.

I had actually intended to write this book for many years; but like some projects, I continued to find excuses to avoid getting started. My son Ben deserves the credit for both pushing me and for encouraging me to get going. He provided me with feedback on my earliest drafts, cheered me along the way, came up with the book's title, and helped provide important feedback on its design elements.

My wife, Catherine, and my daughter, Hannah, supported me—and were graciously willing to overlook their bemusement at my usual all-out method of approaching a task—as I wrote nearly non-stop from the time I started the introduction until I finished the last chapter. Catherine was also one of my editors, proofreading every line of the text, catching my errors (Fundamental #26 – Double-check all work!) and providing valuable input for areas that needed clarification.

I must also thank Ruth Cohen, my other editor, for her painstaking review of my manuscript. Her passion for A+ness matches my own, and together, we reviewed even the smallest of details to be certain this book would be the best I could possibly make it. I also appreciate her permission to break nearly every rule of grammar we learned in school, all in the name of making the book more readable and easier to understand.

I am equally indebted to Sean Sweeney, who worked with me to design the cover for this book, and advised me regarding its interior layout as well. Sean is an artist, a brilliant marketer, and a friend. I appreciate his ability to understand the message I wanted to convey and to translate that message into an effective design.

Lastly, I want to thank the members of my former staff who generously contributed the personal stories that appear throughout this book. In order of appearance, they are: Paul Fetterolf, Bill Kaiser, Bill Lynch, Christine Ament, Ralph Catillo, Jason York, Kurt Hettel, Sharyn Spitznagel, Linda Kozlowski, Maureen Wright, Nora McAdam, Nate Trotman, Kara Badyna, Bonnie Antonelli, Nancy Nessler, Diane Seternus, Christine Gurkin, Tina Lomanno, Beth Delaney, Mindy Johnson, Denise Letourneau, Dennis Boyle, Jeff Ohlstein, Winnie DeAngelo, Bob Flanders, and Doug Barth.

I hope you enjoyed reading Fundamentally *Different* as much as I enjoyed writing it.

David